AF33428

The Picture of Dorian Gray

A Musical Drama

(Based on The Novel by Oscar Wilde)

Book, Music and Lyrics

by

Jack Sharkey & Dave Reiser

SAMUEL FRENCH, INC.

25 WEST 45TH STREET NEW YORK 10036
7623 SUNSET BOULEVARD HOLLYWOOD 90046
80 RICHMOND ST. EAST TORONTO, CANADA M5C 1P1
— LONDON —

THE PICTURE OF DORIAN GRAY

—Cast of Characters—

[NOTE: The number of players in this show is 10—6 males and 4 females—and the various *groups* of characters listed below (such as SYBIL, GWEN and HETTY) are played by the same person.]

1) DORIAN GRAY . . . . .a wealthy young man

2) LORD HENRY WOTTON . . . . .a British nobleman

3) BASIL HALLWARD. . . . . .a renowned artist

4) SYBIL VANE. . . . . .a young actress
   GWEN LANGDON . . . . .a society belle
   HETTY DUVAL . . . . .a lovely noblewoman

5) MRS. VANE . . . . .Sybil's mother
   LADY MARGARET . . . . .Gwen's mother
   OLD GWEN . . . . .an opium addict

6) STAGE MANAGER. . . . . .at Sybil's theatre
   LORD BOYCE . . . . .a British nobleman
   BARTENDER . . . . .at opium den

7) ALAN CAMPBELL . . . . .a medical student
   JAMES VANE . . . . .Sybil's brother

8) THOMAS. . . . . .Dorian's manservant
   BUTLER .at Lady Margaret's
   VICTOR .Thomas's successor

9) LADY ELLERTON . . . . .a British noblewoman
   HAG #1. .friend of Old Gwen

10) LADY BEECHMONT . . . . .a British noblewoman
   HAG #2. .friend of Old Gwen

The play is set in and about London, mid-1800s

THE PICTURE OF DORIAN GRAY

—Synopsis of Scenes and Musical Numbers—

"OVERTURE"

Scene

1) The garden of Basil's house/studio
    "SOMETHING ABOUT A GARDEN" ....Basil,
                                                    Henry
    "THE BEST I'VE EVER DONE" ....Basil
    "THE ONLY THING TO DO"...........Henry,
                                            Basil, Dorian
    "THE PICTURE" ....Dorian
    "SYBIL" ....Dorian

2) Backstage at Sybil's theatre
    "SO DIFF'RENT FROM THE REST" ...Dorian
    "MARRY THE NICE GENTLEMAN" ..James,
                                        Mrs. Vane, Sybil
    "MY PRINCE CHARMING" ....Sybil

3) The dining room at Lady Ellerton's house
    "CONVERSATION"............Henry, Guests

4) A table before the stage of Sybil's theatre
    [No musical number]

5) Backstage at Sybil's theatre and 6) a London
    street/Sybil's stage
    "MY PRINCE CHARMING" (reprise) ....Sybil,
                                                    Dorian
    "THE ONLY THING TO DO"/"I HAVE
        KILLED HIS LOVE"...........Dorian/Sybil

7) Dorian's house (parlor and attic room)
"DID HE SEE?" . . . . Dorian, Thomas

8) The ballroom of Lady Margaret's house and 9)
Lady Margaret's garden
"THE HARMLESS WALTZ" . . . . . Instrumental
"SO DIFF'RENT FROM THE REST"
(reprise) . . . . Dorian, Gwen
[NOTE: Action of the play is continuous, without a
break; if an act-break into two segments is
desired, however, it should come here, and
the following musical number will then
serve in place of an "Entr'Acte" for your
Act Two.]

10) Dorian's house
"INTERLUDE" . . . . Unseen Chorus
"SOMETHING NEW" . . . . Dorian

11) The dining room at Lady Beechmont's house
"THEY SAY" . . . . Quartet of guests
"CONVERSATION" (reprise) . . . . Dorian,
Henry, Guests

12) Dorian's house (featuring the attic)
"PRAYER" . . . . Basil

13) Dorian's house (featuring the parlor)
"I HAVE A TASK" . . . . Dorian, Alan

14) An opium den near the docks
"IN PRAISE OF ADDICTION" . . . . . Old Gwen,
Hags, Bartender
"WHAT'S THE MATTER, CUTIE? . . Old Gwen,
Dorian
"SO IT'S YOU" . . . . James, Dorian
"DIALOGUE" . . . . James, Old Gwen

"I WILL TRACK HIM DOWN" ....James
"EPILOG" ....Old Gwen, Hags

15) The parlor of Dorian's country house
"HETTY" ....Dorian
"THE IDLE RICH" ......Henry, Hetty, Dorian
"TOO GOOD TO BE TRUE"/"SOMETHING
NEW" (reprise) ....Hetty/Dorian

16) A field near the woods on Dorian's estate
"THE SHOOT" ....Ellerton, Beechmont,
Boyce, Dorian

17) Dorian's house (featuring the attic)
"FOR ONCE" ....Dorian
"FINALE" ....Dorian, Hetty

This play is gratefully dedicated to
OSCAR WILDE

poet, novelist, dramatist, lecturer,
raconteur—and frightening philosopher

All settings are suggested, not realistic—openwork, skeletonic sets (a sofa and an open archway and a floating window-frame for the parlor of Dorian's country house, for instance). All backgrounds are dead black, and all visible items are stark white (this includes shrubbery, etc.), best done in reflector-paint such as used on safety-signs, to intensify by contrast the surrounding dark, flat black of the sets. (There should *be* walls, or black draperies, however, so that persons passing through an open doorway will not be visible beyond its edge once they are "out of the room".) The only colors should be on the persons of the players themselves, and these in pastels—lavender, fawn, tan, pink, pale blue, etc. The overall effect of the show should be dreamlike—or nightmarish, as befits the moment—with only the barest hints of reality surrounding the players. With the exception of the sole major set—the parlor and attic of Dorian's house—these can all be lightweight and thus easily movable for the various scene-changes. But that major set, of course, having two levels, should be sturdy enough to support the players without wobbling when they are upstairs.

When the notion of turning Oscar Wilde's novel into a musical drama first struck us, we found ourselves up against something of a mystery. We read the book thoroughly, noticed several scenes that would play eminently well onstage, and several moments that could be rendered in song quite easily—but we also noticed something else, something that began pervading our minds with its downright creepy possiblities:

Oscar Wilde had not only written a novel—he had written what amounted to a *mystery story*—a mystery story *without* the solution! Or—and this is when we started getting goosebumps—*was* there a solution—an implied solution—all clues given—just waiting for the reader to ferret them out and realize the enthralling truth?!

For instance: There was the Alan Campbell character. He enters the story almost abruptly, when Dorian needs help in disposing of the body of a man he murdered. He declares he had vowed never to enter Dorian's house again, so great is his loathing for the man. And he refuses to help Dorian—*until* Dorian shows him a letter which he will mail unless Alan helps him. Alan is shocked, declares that the letter would destroy the woman to whom it is addressed, and agrees to help.

But—and this is only *one* of the maddening moments in the novel—the reader must ask, "*Why* does Alan hate Dorian so? . . . Who *is* this woman? *What* can the letter say that will destroy her?" and one also wonders, after all these years of hating Dorian cannot Alan have contrived some kind of revenge for whatever he has endured at Dorian's hands?

Then—oddly enough—and for no apparently logical reason—Dorian suddenly decides to go to an opium den near the docks. Why? What was his abrupt motivation for going there? Whatever he went for, he does not achieve it in the book since he is met by a man who has vowed to destroy him, and barely escapes with is life.

And what of the girl "Gwendolyn," mentioned many times in the course of the novel, and with allusions to her shame about something dealing with Dorian—but it is never further spelled out.

And finally, in last scene of the novel, Dorian—with no really logical motive—decides all at once to destroy the portrait—and when he makes this attempt—the book suddenly cuts away from the scene, and only describes a terrible scream that rings through the house and arouses all the sleeping servants . . . and when they go up to the attic room, they find the portrait of Dorian as he appeared when a young man—and find Dorian himself turned into the hideous monster the portrait had become.

And just before this climactic event, the novel very briefly mentions a young girl named "Hetty"—a girl Dorian truly cares about—cares about so much that he forsakes his evil ways and abandons her, knowing that his love for her would doom them both.

Well, put all these things together and you have what amounts to an insurmountable mystery . . . or so we thought until, reading and then re-reading the story—the Truth flashed upon us with almost frightening clarity, and we knew we could not rest until we had told the story as it was really meant to be told, with all the clues leading us to the only possible solution of the maddening mysteries: Just who was Gwendolyn? Why did Alan hate Dorian so? Who was the lady to whom the letter was addressed? What was in the letter that would destroy her? What vengenance did Alan enact upon Dorian then? How did this vengeance tie in with his sudden trip to the opium den? What dire information did he have to depart without learning? Who actually was this Hetty that he loved above all other women? And, finally, what *happened* in the attic room when he tried to destroy the painting—what was the *cause* of that terrible scream—and *who* actually was it that *did* the screaming?!

The clues—the answers—had been there all along, staring at us, almost between the lines. And we must hope in all sincerity, that were Oscar Wilde alive today, he would not only approve of our solution to the many mysteries in his novel—he would applaud our discovering the answers, and laying them before the public. We never quite lost the feeling that Oscar was looking over our shoulders as we worked, and nodding his head, and saying, "That's right! You caught it! Good for you!" The entire creative effort has been, you may guess, quite spooky.

But the two of us couldn't be more pleased with the results.

THE AUTHORS
August, 1980

MUSIC—IMPORTANT

Music for this production is available, on a rental and deposit basis.

Rental for use of the music is $10.00 for each performance. We can lend you a piano/vocal score for a period of eight weeks, on receipt of the following:

1. Number of performances and exact performance dates.
2. Rental in full on the music for the entire production.
3. Deposit of $25.00, which is refunded on return to us of the material in good condition immediately after your production. Plus first-class postage and handling charge of $2.50

We cannot fill any order for music unless it is accompanied by remittance as above, as all rental material is handled on a strictly c.o.d. basis.

The Picture of Dorian Gray

SCENE 1

The garden of BASIL HALLWARD'S *house/studio. Curtain-rise finds* BASIL *at work on a large canvas, its back toward us. He works quietly and deftly for a few moments, and then* LORD HENRY WOTTON — *a young man of about* BASIL'S *own age, mid-20s, who is dressed stylishly and just short of foppishly for the period — enters through the open doors behind the other man, who is deep in concentration on his work and does not notice his arrival.* HENRY *pauses just short of speaking, and stares at the canvas in some interest, obviously appreciating what he sees. Then:*

HENRY. Who *is* this young man?!

BASIL. (*looks his way, still partly bemused by his work*) What—? Oh, Harry, it's you. I didn't hear you come out. (*returns to his work*)

HENRY. (*sits on bench, whence he can still study canvas*) Small wonder. When you artists are at work, Basil, I doubt if you could hear a coach-and-four bearing down upon you! . . . But you are evading the issue—tell me who this incredible young god might be! I simply must meet him!

BASIL. (*hesitantly*) I—I don't want you to meet him, Harry.

HENRY. If you imagine that sort of reply will quench my ambition, you know little of human psychology, my

13

friend. If anything, you have now increased my appetite to make his acquaintance.

BASIL. (*stops painting, faces him*) Please don't press the issue, Harry. I don't know quite how to explain my feelings—there is something so . . . so unspoiled, so fresh, so untainted about Dorian Gray that—

HENRY. (*interrupts, triumphantly*) Ah! So that's his name! "Dorian Gray." I rather like it.

BASIL. I didn't mean to let you know it. Harry, we have been friends for many years, and heaven knows *I* am used to you—but a young man such as Dorian— well—you have a certain cynical outlook upon life that I'd rather spare him the acquaintance of . . .

BASIL. (*laughs, amused*) You intrigue me more than ever, Basil! I'd never looked upon myself as anyone's mentor, before—but, do you know—it might prove amusing, introducing this unsullied youth to a keener insight into the nature of things . . .

BASIL. (*more sharply than he intended*) Harry, I forbid it! . . . (*ashamed of his outburst*) That is to say . . .

HENRY. Please don't apologize, there's no need. I deliberately baited you, you know, into that outburst. You are usually so dreadfully solemn.

BASIL. I suppose I am, at that . . . It's not intentional—I just get so caught up in my work—

HENRY. Why are you working out-of-doors, anyhow? Heaven knows, this is a welcome change from the mustiness of your studio, but I'm not entirely certain a background of floral shrubbery suits you.

BASIL. It's this painting—it's Dorian—there's something—well—something of the loveliness of nature—of spring—of freshness—about him, that made this seem the only logical setting in which to paint him.

HENRY. A garden is best enjoyed peering through a window from indoors, where one can appreciate the panorama of color and design without subjecting oneself to attacks by insects, merciless sunlight, and soggy shoes.

BASIL. Harry, you have no soul.

HENRY. I have something better. I have sensitivity.

BASIL. Even so—this is the perfect setting for my painting . . . (*MUSIC   intros, and he sings:*) There's something about a garden!

HENRY. (*overlapping him in song*) Enjoying it isn't easy!

BASIL. See there how the leaves are turning green!

HENRY. Turning sensitive stomachs queasy!

BASIL. Eruptions of fragrant roses!

HENRY. Esthetic'ly bad for noses!

BASIL. Suspended below the sky serene!

HENRY. Skies are really rather plain!

BASIL. There's something about a garden!

HENRY. Entangled by vine and bramble!

BASIL. All splendors of nature at their best!

HENRY. At their bestial worst, I'd gamble!

BASIL. Believe me, I dearly love it!

HENRY. It's easy to weary of it!

BASIL. It's truly a place where one can rest!

HENRY. One can rest assured of rain!

BASIL. Just feel of the textured ivy!

HENRY. I've an allergy that precludes it!

BASIL. You distress me with your conniving!

HENRY. I've a temp'rament that exudes it!

BASIL. It's really a lovely garden!

HENRY. Enchanting, I'm sure, to others!

BASIL. There's beauty abundantly in sight!

HENRY. I agree, in spite of the fact it smothers!

BASIL. There's nothing to please you, is there!

HENRY. Is there anything pales like pleasure?

BASIL. You're missing the joys of life!

HENRY. The joys of life are trite!

BASIL. You don't mean a word!

HENRY. You're right!

BASIL. (*laughs, but shakes his head sadly*) There, now! That's the very sort of thing I *don't* want Dorian exposed to!

HENRY. Oh, but my dear friend—

BASIL. *I* know you talk solely for effect, and don't mean a syllable! But a young impressionable man— (*stops, as* DORIAN GRAY—*a young man whose male vitality is just barely able to prevent one seeing him as beautiful—enters garden toward rear of bench where* HENRY *sits*) Oh. Dorian. You're early . . .

HENRY. (*galvanized by the sound of the name, stands and turns*) So! We meet at last, Dorian Gray! I feared Basil was going to deny me that pleasure!

BASIL. (*trapped, does the polite thing*) Dorian, this is Lord Henry Wotton. Harry, the young man I told you of, Dorian Gray.

(*the two men smile and bow slightly to one another*)

DORIAN. I am honored, Lord Henry.

HENRY. "Harry," please. I only use my title when there's no other way to get a good table at a fashionable restaurant.

DORIAN. "Harry," then. But—Basil—did I understand that you didn't wish me to make Lord Henry's acquaintance?

BASIL. (*pause; then:*) No, I did not. At least—not just yet. Harry is so . . . of the world and you're so untouched by it, yet . . .

HENRY. Ah, but it's only a matter of time, you know. All his freshness, all his incredible beauty—

DORIAN. You embarrass me, Harry—!

HENRY. But it's true. You have youth, Dorian. It's really the only thing worth having. What a pity it must be wasted on the young.

DORIAN. (*amused*) I don't think I need worry about aging for a *few* more years, at least.

HENRY. Ah, but you should, my boy, you should. Because, sooner than you imagine, your beauty is doomed to the same fate as the rose's. First the shape goes, then the texture, then the color—

BASIL. Really, Harry, you will render our young friend totally despondent!

HENRY. No, dear Basil, I will not, because all of my trenchant warnings will be couched in the most amusing terms, and if I render him anything, it will be a delightful afternoon!

BASIL. (*impatient to return to his work*) Oh, very well, very well! By all means, amuse him, while I finish up some of the background-work on the canvas—and Dorian, I charge you, enjoy every word he says—but don't believe a fragment of it!

DORIAN. (*laughs*) You have my word, Basil.

HENRY. (*links arms with* DORIAN) Then let us stroll down toward that lilac bush over near the garden gate. I need something for my buttonhole that will overcome the odor of Basil's turpentine!

(DORIAN *and* HENRY *stroll off;* BASIL *continues to work for a few more moments, then steps back, scanning the canvas; he seems magnetized, enrapt, and slowly lowers his brush to his side, never taking his gaze from the painting, as MUSIC intros, and:*)

BASIL. (*sings*)
I can't get over it! What am I seeing, here?
How could one fail to love the beauty of this being, here?
Each brush-stroke flowing, ev'ry feature glowing,
Warm and wise and knowing, like a living thing!
Can it be my hand has wrought a miracle?
Of all my works, what magic stirs this one?

Here at last I find my crowning glory in
Dorian . . . the best I've ever done . . .

(*He is still standing there, staring, as* DORIAN *and*
HENRY *re-enter, the latter affixing a sprig of lilac
to his lapel;* BASIL *breaks from his trance as*
DORIAN *laughs*)

DORIAN. Truly, Harry, you are outrageous!

BASIL. What terrible things has he been saying to
you, Dorian?

DORIAN. Well—

BASIL. Here, now, just stand there, where you've
been posing for me—I have just a detail or two about
your face that I must set right . . .

HENRY. (*while* BASIL *positions* DORIAN *and returns
to the canvas*) I do hope you mean the painted face, and
not the actual one? There's not a feature of his I'd ever
want to alter. (*will sit again on bench, where he can
watch both men*) I was merely regaling Dorian with the
tale of that certain lady of our acquaintance, Lady
Bentley, the one who is so keen on assisting the lower
classes that she has absolutely no time for personal
hygeine.

BASIL. (*becoming absorbed in his work*) Harry, you
do the lady a disservice.

HENRY. Not as great a disservice as the scent of her
breath does to the world at large. I was finally forced to
mention it to her.

BASIL. (*distracted from the canvas for a moment*)
Harry, that is a dreadful breach of decorum, even for
you!

HENRY. Why should telling the truth offend anyone?
I rather thought I was doing her a kindness, since no one
else of her acquaintance had apparently taken her aside
to do so.

DORIAN. But surely—that is—when you told the lady, what was her reply?

HENRY. What one might expect from a person engaged in social work: She took it quite calmly, smiled, and said that her breath was not *bad*—it was merely *misunderstood!*

(DORIAN *and* BASIL *both laugh*)

On her subsequent birthday, I sent her a lovely lacquer box filled with breath mints! Plus a charming note which in the most gallant terms informed her that any notion of romance between us must be forsaken!

BASIL. Harry, you didn't!

HENRY. My dear Basil, one simply has to be firm with women in such matters, or they will fantasize the most incredible things about one. These days, to simply lean across the table to pass the cream convinces a women that you have decided to become her lifelong slave.

DORIAN. (*maintaining his pose as* BASIL *paints away*) But really, Harry—breath mints?

HENRY. I considered the gift my duty to the noses of decent society.

(BASIL *and* DORIAN *laugh, MUSIC intros, and* HENRY *sings:*)

It was the only thing to do!
A lady must not misconstrue
A tete-a-tete as lifelong passion once
You terminate the rendezvous!
To merely take her out to dine
Is not to crave a concubine!
And yet a lady thinks
Just because you buy her drinks
That your future interlinks
Heart-to-heart forever
When the notion never
Even crossed your mind!
As you go on through life, you'll find

It's a conclusion she's always jumping to!
And so, to simply kid her,
Then bid her toodle-oo,
Is the only thing a gentleman can do!
   BASIL. (*spoken*) You mean a cad!
   DORIAN. (*spoken*) Is he truly all that bad?
   HENRY. (*continues singing:*)
It was the only thing to do!
When a romance is through, it's through!
Eight-forty-five she speaks
Of love that reeks
Of tedium by ten-oh-two!
True love at lunch is fine, if we
Can break it off in time for tea!
   BASIL. Don't listen, Dorian!
   HENRY. Basil's so Victorian!
   DORIAN. But I find his story enthralling!
   HENRY. Conversation is my calling!
   BASIL. (*who has not stopped working since song*
began)
Though I can't say I approve,
At any rate, dear boy don't move
Until I've captured that blush upon your cheek!
(spoken)
Don't speak!
   HENRY. (*continuing song*)
Then I shall go on voicing my anti-social view!
   BASIL.
It's tommyrot!
How does he dare!?
   DORIAN.
Any yet, he's got
An honest air!
   HENRY.
Well, true or not,
What else is there to do!?

(BASIL *and* DORIAN *laugh, and* BASIL *lowers his brush*)

DORIAN. I'm sorry, Basil. I shouldn't have moved.

BASIL. No-no, it's quite all right. The portrait is completed.

(*Starts turning canvas on the easel, toward us, as* HENRY *comes to his feet, and* DORIAN *moves closer to view it; then we see it: It is* DORIAN *in the flesh, as we are now seeing him, a truly magnificent picture of youth, against a brilliant background of flowers and blossom-laden boughs and brilliant blue sky; the trio stands in silence for a moment; then:*)

Well? Do you approve, Dorian?

DORIAN. Approve?! Basil—it's—it's like looking into a mirror! Am I truly so handsome as that?

HENRY. You are today, at any rate. How miraculous is art—to capture the heart of beauty before it fades forever . . . This picture will always show you at the height of your youth . . . even as the years slowly corrode and destroy what you are, this monument to your beauty will remain thus, unchanged.

DORIAN. How I wish it could be otherwise . . . that the picture could change and grow old, and I could remain this way forever . . .!

BASIL. Ah well, that is not the way of things in this life, more's the pity.

HENRY. All this outdoor romping in the shrubbery has created a vast thirst inside me, Basil. Are you still possessed of that most excellent Napoleon brandy I sent you at Christmastime?

BASIL. You know I am, Harry. You only sent it to me so that you could come over here and drink it without your wife standing by your side counting the glassfuls.

HENRY. (*links arms with* BASIL, *starts toward doors*) How I wish that weren't true!

(*as* BASIL *laughs*)

Coming, Dorian—?

DORIAN. (*still staring at the painting*) In—in a moment, Harry . . . I just want to look—a little longer—

BASIL. As you wish. I'll pour you a brandy, nonetheless, before Harry finishes the entire bottle!

(BASIL *and* HENRY *exit into house;* DORIAN *continues to stare at painting as MUSIC intros, and:*)

DORIAN. (*sings*)
The picture! No part of it can time disarrange!
Isn't it strange! Time cannot change
The picture! Like gazing in a mirror:
Declining years seem nearer,
And what I am much dearer to me!
Could I but see
Within its depths the ravages of age there,
Magic'ly encaged there!
Then let time take its toll!
For this, I'd surrender my soul . . . !

(*he is still standing there as MUSIC fades*)

BASIL. (*appears in doorway, holding two snifters of brandy*) Dorian—? Your brandy is waiting. Better have it before Harry commandeers all the goblets.

DORIAN. (*breaks from his enrapt, troubled mood*) What—? Oh, yes, of course . . . but . . . I wonder—might I have it out here?

HENRY. (*appears beside* BASIL, *carrying own snifter*) There, now, what did I tell you, Basil! He can't bear to tear himself away from that portrait. I find this moment utterly fascinating . . .

(*during speech,* HENRY *will move out to seat himself on bench,* BASIL *will come a few paces outside doors but remain standing, and* DORIAN *will remain where he is*)

It's like having a front-row seat at the debut of Narcissus finding and falling in love with his reflection in that ancient pool. I must say, though, that were I as gifted in aspect as Dorian, I could quite easily become enamored of myself above all others.

BASIL. As if you hadn't already done so! (*hands one snifter to* DORIAN, *then sits beside* HENRY)

HENRY. (*to* DORIAN) He's quite right, you know. Would that all my companions could be half so charming as I. Dorian, will you dine with me tonight?

DORIAN. I should enjoy that very much, Harry. (*raises his snifter to drink, then lowers it*) Oh—but—I've only just remembered—I cannot. I have a previous engagement. (*slightly self-conscious*) There's—this girl. Sybil Vane. I only met her yesterweek, but—well—

BASIL. Dorian—you don't mean to say you've fallen in love—?

HENRY. Now, then, Dorian, see how you've disappointed our host. An artist always feels that anyone he selects to portray should spend the rest of his life in mindless devotion to him.

BASIL. (*though this shot has been right on the mark*) Don't be ridiculous, Harry. (*hastily pretends to be absorbed in sipping brandy*)

HENRY. But do tell me about this Sybil Vane—it's certainly a lovely name.

DORIAN. (*moving his way, waxing enthusiastic*) And eminently suitable to the girl who bears it. She's unlike any other woman I have ever met.

HENRY. From a lad of your tender years, such a declaration is somewhat lacking in magnitude.

BASIL. (*unhappy*) Do you mean to marry her, Dorian?

HENRY. Oh let us hope not. Nothing can ruin a romance faster than marriage. But tell me about her, Dorian. Who is she?

DORIAN. She is an actress.

BASIL. An actress? I have never heard of her.

DORIAN. No one has. People will someday, however. She is a genius.

HENRY. My dear boy, no woman is a genius. Women are a decorative sex. They never have anything to say, but they say it charmingly. Women represent the triumph of matter over minds, just as men represent the triumph of mind over morals.

BASIL. Harry, how can you!

HENRY. It is quite true, Basil. There are only five women in London worth having a conversation with, and two of them cannot be admitted into decent society. But tell me of your actress, Dorian. Where did you come across her?

DORIAN. At an absurd little theatre on the east side, with great flaring gas jets and gaudy playbills. They were playing Shakespeare, and I was curious to see how the Bard might fare in such an outrageous locale. The next thing I knew, to my own surprised amusement, I was paying a guinea for the privilege of sitting at a table directly before the stage, with a horridly vulgar drop-scene staring me in the face, all cupids and cornucopias, like a third-rate wedding cake. When I saw that the play was *Romeo and Juliet*—and it was not easy to tell, in their rendition, what with Romeo being an elderly gentleman with corkblackened eyebrows and a figure like a beer barrel—I very nearly took my leave, fearing my incipient laughter would distress the players. But then, Henry, Juliet entered and all urgings toward mirth departed.

BASIL. Your Sybil, I take it?

DORIAN. Oh, if you could have seen her, Basil, you would know something of what I feel . . . Imagine a girl, hardly seventeen years of age, with a little flowerlike face, a small Grecian head with plaited coils of dark brown hair, eyes that were violet wells of passion, lips that were like the petals of a rose . . . She was the loveliest thing I had ever seen in my life.

BASIL. Are you certain that you have fallen in love with Sybil, or with Juliet?

DORIAN. Ah, but that's just it, my friends! They change the program nightly. Each encounter with her is new . . . she is Juliet, then Rosalind, then Ophelia, then Hermia . . all the heroines of history in one!

HENRY. Bravo, Dorian! The only thing worth loving is an actress. But tell me, Dorian, when is she Sybil Vane?

DORIAN. Never.

HENRY. I congratulate you.

DORIAN. Harry, you don't understand her. She knows nothing of life. She thinks of everything as a part of a play. Even myself. She thinks I look like a prince, and calls me Prince Charming.

HENRY. Better and better. In affairs such as this, it is always vital never to reveal one's real name.

DORIAN. Harry, Sybil Vane is sacred! I could not call our relationship an affair!

BASIL. But surely, Dorian—an actress—from the east side . . .

DORIAN. You shall judge for yourself. Will you come with me, tonight—the two of you—to see her? Then you shall know all of your arguments are nonsense.

BASIL. I might manage tomorrow night . . . Harry?

HENRY. It could prove amusing, at that. Very well, Dorian, we shall come. (*rises*) And now, since the air is turning a bit chilly, I shall go indoors and see what comfort remains in the brandy bottle.

BASIL. (*rises, will follow* HENRY *through doors, during:*) I'd best keep an eye on him, or he'll be starting on the cooking sherry next. Coming, Dorian?

DORIAN. No, I cannot. I'll let myself out by the garden gate. It's already past time for me to be starting for the theatre.

BASIL. As you wish . . . Oh! (*pauses just short of exit*) About the picture—

DORIAN. Just have it sent around to my house in the morning, Basil. I really cannot concern myself with it now. (*hands* BASIL *emptied snifter*) I thank you for your hospitality—and the introduction to Harry.

BASIL. I'm not so sure that is something for which you will always be grateful.

(DORIAN *laughs;* BASIL *starts indoors*)

Till tomorrow night, then.

DORIAN. Till tomorrow. Tomorrow—and Sybil.

(*He will stand there, not moving, but the garden setting and all its accouterments will fade slowly away, leaving him the only thing in bright view against the darkness, as MUSIC intros, and he sings, rapturously:*)

Sweet Juliet, I implore you!
Dear Desdemona, be mine!
Whoever you are, you're divine!
What variety!
Be my Rosalind, or you
Can be Bianca so fair,
So long as your love I can share!
Your talents I'll tally, as daily we dally,
For in you I find, dear, an endless wealth of womankind!
Dear days ahead, I adore you for all you're going to be!
No one dare dispute you're the fabulous future I see
For Sybil and me! Ah, yes . . .

(*MUSIC softens and sweetens and saddens*)

Sybil is a creature of such wide variety,
As I think of her and see what she seems to me . . .
Sybil is a flower sweet and rare . . .

Sybil is that pearl of awesome price beyond compare . . .
Yet what flow'r or precious gem could hope to rival her
   perfection?
Virginal and trusting, with the dusting of the stars
Within her gentle smiling eyes . . . Dare my hopes arise
To this sacred shrine . . . hoping she might agree soon to
   be mine?
Forever mine . . .

(LIGHTS FADE - end of scene)

SCENE 2

Backstage at SYBIL's *theatre.* DORIAN *remains in our
view from preceding scene as Lights Come Up on
what is mostly a dressing-room area, but partly a
backstage corridor, in which* DORIAN *is now standing. The dressing room is indicated by a mirrored
dressing-table, a large trunk, and a rack of
costumes; it has two doors, one to the corridor, and
one to a room—unseen—beyond the area of the
dressing-table.* SYBIL *is seated at this table, and is
fully as lovely as described in the preceding scene.
She is in Shakespearian costume, but is in the process of removing a headpiece—a tiara, feathered
cap, or whatever—so that we know she has just
come offstage.* DORIAN *moves to the door and
knocks lightly.* SYBIL *turns slightly, but remains
seated as she sets headpiece down and:*

SYBIL. Yes? Who's there?
DORIAN. Someone not fit to worship at your feet!
SYBIL. (*springs up, rushes to door with a happy
laugh, flings it open*) My Prince Charming! You honor
me with your presence, sire! (*does a little curtsey*)

DORIAN. (*laughs, and as she rises, takes her in his arms*) You never tire of your little game, do you! Would that I were truly a prince—I should ask you to reign at my side forever.

SYBIL. What, a common actress on the royal throne? The kingdom would be in an uproar!

DORIAN. Then I should abandon both throne and kingdom. You are more to me than all the pomp and splendor that ever was!

(*Kisses her ardently; she returns his ardor, but then pulls gently away from him, and turns her back*)

SYBIL. Then you agree I am not suited for the royal house?

DORIAN. (*moves to her, embraces her waist from behind*) There is no royal house worthy of you. Principalities pale before your beauty, your radiance, your—

SYBIL. (*Interrupts, but remains in his arms, resting her head back upon his shoulder*) Sire, you will turn my head with your flattery!

DORIAN. But it is not flattery I utter. The merest truth about you would only seem flattery to lesser women.
(*MUSIC intros, and he sings:*)
Your eyes, like candles in the mist . . .
Give rise to feeling too appealing to resist!
Are you the sweet conclusion of my quest?
You are so diff'rent . . so diff'rent from the rest!
(*she slowly turns in his embrace to face him, during:*)
Your arms, whose promise of embrace
Alarms my heart as fingers start to interlace!
Enfold me, then, and hold me to your breast . . .
You are so diff'rent . . . so diff'rent from the rest!
(*she contentedly embraces him, her cheek upon his chest*)
My dream of ecstasy I now realize!

I seem at last to be held fast in paradise . . . !
Your kiss . . . Oh, answer my appeal
For this sweet pleasure! Who can measure what I feel?
This longing may be wrong, but dare I leave it unex-
pressed . . .
           (*she is looking up at him, now*)
To one so diff'rent . . . so diff'rent from the rest . . . ?!
           (*they kiss again, gently, sweetly, briefly*)
SYBIL. (*releases him, moves to dressing-table*) Such
lovely things you say, sire. They bring tears to my eyes.
DORIAN. (*moving after her*) The words are for you
alone—I shall never speak them to another. (*turns her
to face him*) Sybil—I am asking you to become my wife.
SYBIL. (*startled, uncertain*) Oh, but sire . . .
DORIAN. Please. No more play-acting. Tell me what
is in your heart.
SYBIL. May I—may I have time—just a little time—to
ponder your most generous offer . . . ?
DORIAN. Of course, my love. You shall have until
tomorrow, at this same time. I shall be here with two
friends—your acceptance will be the soaring culmina-
tion to our evening's delight at your performance.
SYBIL. You seem very certain what my reply shall be.
DORIAN. When heart speaks to heart, there can be no
uncertainty. (*kisses her lightly on the lips*) Now, then, to
your restful bed, dearest darling, to think upon what I
have begged of you, tonight. I shall see you here again,
tomorrow. (*backs toward door*) Goodnight, my love.
SYBIL. Goodnight, goodnight, my prince . . .

(DORIAN *exits, moves down corridor and vanishes;*
    SYBIL *turns toward mirror, and is staring*
    breathlessly at her reflection therein as MRS. VANE
    and JAMES VANE—*a faded and drab woman and*
    Sybil's tall, roughly dressed brother—enter from
    room beyond dressing-table)

MRS. VANE. There! I knew it! You're going to marry him! All our troubles are past!

SYBIL. Mother! You should be ashamed, listening at doors!

JAMES. There is no shame in watching over your welfare, Sybil. I don't trust this "Prince Charming" of yours, with his fancy airs and fine manners—!

SYBIL. James, don't! You have never even met him!

JAMES. Lay the blame for that upon our mother! She would not let me so much as open the door an inch for a look at your fine gentleman!

MRS. VANE. How did I dare?! One creak of the hinges, and the magical moment would have been shattered! But her fine gentleman is as good as captured, bound, and handed over!

SYBIL. I have not yet given him my answer, Mother.

JAMES. And what will your answer be, dear sister? Remember, our own father was as fine a gentleman as your own—and he never saw fit to either wed our mother nor remain with her after my birth!

SYBIL. My Prince Chaming is not like that. He is good, and fine, and—

JAMES. (*clasps her by the shoulders*) I wish my ship did not sail in the morning. I should remain here, and see that you are properly looked after!

SYBIL. Mother is here.

JAMES. Fat lot of good that will do you! One mention of money, and she would sell you to an arab!

MRS. VANE. You break my heart, James.

JAMES. (*laughs fondly*) Mother, you have no heart, and you know it! I am concerned with my sister's future happiness—all you care about is your pocketbook!

MRS. VANE. Well . . . where's the harm in her marrying into money? If she loves the man, the money is just a lovely extra frosting on the wedding-cake!

SYBIL. Mother, do not speak of weddings just yet. I must think this matter through.

JAMES. Ah! Then you *do* have doubts about your gentleman!

SYBIL. What? Oh, no, never of him. Of myself—of my own worthiness to wed him.

JAMES. You are worth ten of him, Sybil.

MRS. VANE. My sentiments, precisely! Oh, Sybil, my darling, make your poor old mother's declining years happy ones, please!

(*MUSIC intros, and she sings:*)
Marry the nice gentleman!
Tell'm the answer's yes!
Long as he finds you a fabulous jewel, just
Give'm the go-ahead! Sybil, if you will just
Marry the nice gentleman,
Think of our happiness!
Nevermore begging the neighborhood grocer to
Give us more credit! So don't you say "No, sir!" to
Anything he may ask for!
Feed'm your charmingest glances!
Put yourself to the task, for
We really need the finances!
Think of the glorious morning in June
You're there at his side,
Dressed as a bride!
Then when you come back from your honeymoon
To your house in the square,
I will be there!
(SYBIL *and* JAMES *exchange an amused look; they've heard their mother's social ambitions before*)
How can you wonder if you should refuse the man?
Think what a fool
Thing that would be!
Fiscally speaking, we truly could use the man,
If you'll

Only
Marry the nice gentleman!
Tell'm you acquiesce!
Give'm your hand in a marvelous marriage,
And I will arrive in the very next carriage!
    SYBIL. Prince Charming!
    JAMES. And you, dear!
    MRS. VANE. And little old me!
    SYBIL/JAMES.What a fabulous future I'm/you're certain to see!
    MRS. VANE. As your family burden increases to three!
    SYBIL/JAMES. (*give one another resigned-to-Mother looks as they each flick a thumb over their shoulders toward* MRS. VANE, *on:*)
And you know who the third one'll be!
    MRS. VANE. (*oblivious, hitches up her skirts and does a jig of anticipatory delight throughout remainder of song*)
Oh, won't you
Marry the nice gentleman! . . .

(*she will continue singing entire song again, as* JAMES
        and SYBIL *sing, contrapuntally, to her or to one
        another, as the lyric dictates, while she dances*)

    JAMES. As her brother, I still contend
We know nothing of her fine friend!
    SYBIL. James, don't be alarmed! All is well!
He means me no harm! I can tell
By the touch of his hand—!
    JAMES.
You could be wrong!
    SYBIL.
By the sound of his voice—!
    JAMES.
Listen to me!

SYBIL.
By his manner so grand—!
JAMES.
You don't belong—!
SYBIL.
I can only rejoice!
JAMES.
Can't you see
That there could be danger,
Sister so dear—
SYBIL.
Nonsense, nonsense!
JAMES.
From this stranger!
SYBIL.
You needn't fear!
JAMES.
Won't you hear?
SYBIL.
I've been so lonely!
Don't be unkind!
JAMES.
Sybil, you're blind!
SYBIL.
True love I'll find . . .
JAMES.
I wouldn't really mind . . .
JAMES/SYBIL. (*along with* MRS. VANE, *who has reached same part of lyric*) If you'll only—
SYBIL.
Give us your blessing!
JAMES.
Just keep'm guessing
Till I return!
SYBIL.
I cannot spurn
The promise of eternal love from . . .

MRS. VANE. (*repeating happily as she jigs out to room beyond*) Marry'm now! Marry'm now! Marry'm now! Marry'm now! . . .

JAMES. (*following her out, expostulating, waving his arms*)
Mother, for the love of heaven!
Mother, for the love of heaven!

(*as* SYBIL *finishes her own phrase, oblivious to both of them:*)

SYBIL. My . . . Prince . . . Charming . . . ! (*they are gone; song has finished, but NEW MUSIC intros, and, alone in the center of the room,* SYBIL *rhapsodizes:*)
My Prince Charming!
No make-believe lover—he's real!
Although I can't see
Why he's chosen me,
I know deep inside how I feel.
My Prince Charming
Is coming to take me away!
I love all he's planned!
I'll give him my hand
Tomorrow, right after the play!
He's a gentleman, with wealth beyond compare;
He's a handsome one, with features fine and fair.
But if he'd turn ugly, or tawdry, or poor—
I know I'd still love him, perhaps even more!
My Prince Charming, in shining white armor he came.
Though we've barely met, I love him—and yet—
I don't even know his real name! But that doesn't
    matter,
'Cause I know he always will be my Prince Charming to
    me!

(LIGHTS FADE — end of scene)

Scene 3

The dining room at Lady Ellerton's *house.* Lady
Ellerton *is seated at the head of the table. Also
seated there in other spots are* Lady Beechmont,
Alan Campbell, Basil, Henry, Dorian *and*
Lord Boyce. *The lord and ladies are just leaving
middle-age behind, but* Alan *is as young and
handsome as the other young men at the table.
Seating is optional, but* Dorian *should be beside*
Henry. *[NOTE: This setting is precisely the same
one that will be used in a later scene at* Lady
Beechmont's *house; the only seating difference
there will be that the two ladies will switch places.]
The accouterments are the table and chairs, a
chandelier overhead, and the food and drink upon
the table. Those not speaking are busily eating and
drinking and simulating unheard conversation with
the other non-speakers.*

DORIAN. I do wish they'd all eat faster. I must not be
late to the theatre.

HENRY. Patience, Dorian, patience. We have ample
time. Trust me.

ALAN. The play must be marvelous, to provoke such
discomfiture in you.

DORIAN. Not the play, Alan, the actress who stars in
it. She is a marvel. I have hopes that—well—

ALAN. You are in love. I can tell. We have something
in common. Are you acquainted with Lady Margaret's
daughter Gwen?

HENRY. *I* have met her, yes. A charming girl—if a bit
imperious.

ALAN. She does tend to impose her will on me a
bit—but I adore it.

HENRY. A stubborn girl is always delightful—before marriage. Afterward—

DORIAN. Harry, I won't hear anything against marriage tonight! No matter how amusingly you put it!

HENRY. But Dorian, you are so young to become someone's husband! There is so much in life for you to yet experience. Men only marry because they are tired; women because they are curious; both are disappointed.

BASIL. Dorian, don't believe a word of what he says! Harry is an eminently happy married man himself!

HENRY. Only because my wife and I so seldom see one another. She has her life, I have mine; it is a charming arrangement for both of us.

ALAN. It won't be that way with me and Gwen. Dorian, you simply must meet her. There will be a party tomorrow night, at Lady Margaret's. Gwen and I intend to announce our engagement then. Will you come, as my guest?

DORIAN. I should enjoy that, Alan, but unfortunately, my own heart is bound up in its own tomorrows.

ALAN. Well, if you should change your mind—please do come.

HENRY. Yes, Dorian, you should go. You could bring your actress. She could recite *The Charge of the Light Brigade.*

BASIL. Harry, that is cruel.

HENRY. Well, one must say *something* to relieve the tedious conversation one normally must listen to at these affairs.

DORIAN. I find no tedium in pleasant chatter.

HENRY. Then you have not been using your ears. And I dearly wish I had not been using mine!

(*MUSIC intros, and:*)

BOYCE. (*sings*)
Parliament will be in session in a week or so—

ELLERTON.
Discussing Lady Astor's indiscretion off in Monaco.
  BASIL.
I hear the new prime minister
Has promised that within his term
Of office nothing sinister
Shall cause his overthrow.
  BEECHMONT.
Friday I'll endure a tea
At Lady Anne's affair
Collecting clothing for the poor and needy.
Will I see you there?
  ELLERTON.
I do hate to forswear a tea
Providing clothes for charity,
But I have nothing fit to wear!
  BEECHMONT.
This is so delicious! Will you share the recipe?
  HENRY.
If she's referring to the fish,
I'd rather bury it at sea!

(ALAN *and* DORIAN *laugh lightly, amused by this and
    future interjections by* HENRY)

  ELLERTON.
Now, would you like to test a lovely
Wine I must confess I love?
  HENRY.
Thus damning the digestion of
Unwary bourgeoisie!
  BOYCE.
How do you suppose the pound
Will fare in foreign trade,
Now that the lower house is honor-bound
To back a Swiss blockade?

BEECHMONT.
Last month in France, I hesitate
To tell how much I overate!
    HENRY.
Her foreign pounds are quite self-made!
    ELLERTON.
Daring fashions ev'ry autumn
Fill me with despair,
For I am sure that if I ever brought 'em,
Gentlemen would stare!
    HENRY.
She fears the fashion for the fall,
Yet if she entered in the altogether,
Not a gentleman would even leave his chair!
    BASIL.
Why discourse by cataloguing virtues, one by one?
    ELLERTON.
Illicit sex, divorce and secret sin
Are really much more fun!
    ALL.
A dose of degradation
Puts a kick in conversation
When it's done in a delightful way!
Though we betray each other's flaws,
It's really quite all right, because
We never hear a word we say!

(the song is over; DORIAN rises)

DORIAN. Lady Ellerton, I thank you for a delightful dinner, but now I must beg your indulgence to depart, as I have a rather pressing engagement.
    HENRY. (rises) And so do I!
    BASIL. (rises) And I!
    ALAN. (sotto voce to the TRIO) I certainly wish I had!
    ELLERTON. La! What a shame! I am devastated. I had so much to talk about! Ah, well, if you must, you must!

(TRIO *starts out, as she rings small bell for servant*)
Now, let us get to that wine!
  BOYCE. Good show, old girl!

(LIGHTS FADE - end of scene)

SCENE 4

A table before the stage of SYBIL's *theatre.* DORIAN,
    HENRY *and* BASIL *are still visible from the last
    scene, and they move to that table, now, and sit,
    glancing up at the hideous dropcloth earlier
    described by* DORIAN.

HENRY. Dorian, I expect your young lady *will* be a
marvel; that *dropcloth* is certainly everything you
claimed! Of course, anyone would look marvelous in
comparison to it!
  BASIL. Hush, Harry! You must give the young lady a
fair chance.
  DORIAN. A pity we arrived late. But I believe we shall
be just in time for her balcony scene . . .
  HENRY. If she is as talented as you said, we shall not
miss what preceded it. And if she is not, we shall have
been done a mercy.
  BASIL. Henry, be still, the curtain is rising!
                (*as dropcloth starts upward:*)
  HENRY. If our luck holds, it will stick up there and
never return to view.
  DORIAN. Harry, please!
  HENRY. Oh, very well, very well!

(*cloth is out of sight, now, and Lights Come Up on
    SYBIL, in the costume of Juliet, on a somewhat
    tacky balcony*)

SYBIL. (*her interpretation is flat, emotionless, dreadful*) "Oh, Romeo, Romeo! Wherefore art thou Romeo? . . ."

(*the* TRIO *react to this horror,* DORIAN *with shock and shame,* HENRY *and* BASIL *with embarrassment, as she continues:*)

"Deny thy father, and refuse thy name; or, if thou wilt not, be but sworn my love—" (*at this point, she sees* DORIAN, *waves cheerily at him and winks, then gets back "into character" for:*) "—and I'll no longer be a Capulet."

DORIAN. (*pounding the heel of his fist firmly—but not too noisily—onto the tabletop*) She is dreadful! She is atrocious! She is worse than bad, she is vile!

SYBIL. (*continuing quite poorly*) "What's in a name? That which we call a rose by any other name would smell as sweet . . ." (*she will continue apparently speaking, but in silence, over:*)

BASIL. My dear Dorian, anyone can have a bad night—perhaps the excitement of the evening—your proposal of marriage last night—

DORIAN. I am appalled. And ashamed. To have brought you to see this travesty—!

HENRY. Now-now, Dorian, whatever her histrionic merits, I can certainly see that she is as lovely as you described her. What does it matter if—

DORIAN. Go! Leave me! I cannot bear your pity! I must be by myself . . . I must think . . .

(HENRY *and* BASIL *rise*)

BASIL. (*still trying to comfort him*) She is, as Harry has observed, quite charming a young lady . . .

(*looks helplessly at* HENRY, *but he firmly shakes his head as if to say "This is not the moment, Basil," and so he sighs and starts following* HENRY *out, on:*)

Goodnight, dear friend. I beg you—do not take this too strongly—

DORIAN. (*abruptly comes to his feet*) No, wait. I'm coming with you. I abandon her. I never wish to see her again—

(*Lights Fade on table/stage, but* TRIO *is still visible*)

—hear her discordant voice—feel the touch of her grasping hand—! To think that I was ever pleased to have such a person adore me!

HENRY. Being adored is a nuisance. Women treat us as Humanity treats its gods. They worship us and are forever bothering us to do something for them.

BASIL. Harry, this is not the time for jesting. Women give men the very gold of their lives!

HENRY. But they invariably want it back in such very small change. Some wise Frenchman once observed that women inspire us to create masterpieces, and always prevent us from carrying them out.

BASIL. Harry, you must not speak so of that poor girl.

HENRY. Oh, very well, I apologize. Dorian, she is quite beautiful, but she can't act. Let us go.

BASIL. Wait, Harry, I entreat you. Dorian, perhaps Miss Vane is ill. Perhaps if we returned some other night—

DORIAN. She is not ill. She has altered. Last night she was a great artist. Tonight she was commonplace, mediocre, worse than dreadful.

BASIL. Dorian, don't talk like that about anyone you love. Love is a more wonderful thing than Art.

HENRY. But both are simply forms of initation. Let us go, Dorian, it is not good for one's morals to see bad acting. Besides, I don't suppose you will want your wife to act, so what does it matter that she plays Juliet like a wooden doll? She is very lovely, and if she knows as little about life as she does of acting, she will be a delightful experience. Come with us to the club, and we shall drink to the beauty of Sybil Vane. She *is* quite beautiful. What more can you want?

DORIAN. No. Leave me. I must be alone. My heart is breaking.

BASIL. Yes, Harry. Let us go.

(*the two men go off;* DORIAN *remains in place, head bowed*)

(LIGHTS FADE - end of scene)

SCENE 5

The corridor/dressing-room area backstage. SYBIL *is just completing a costume-change, hastily. The corridor door is open.* DORIAN, *who has remained visible to us since end of last scene, enters behind her and stands staring at her until she senses him and turns.*

SYBIL. (*much amused*) How badly I am acting, tonight!

DORIAN. (*amazed at her attitude*) Horribly. Horribly. It was dreadful. Are you ill? You have no idea what I suffered.

SYBIL. But—darling—you understand why, don't you?

DORIAN. Understand?

SYBIL. Why I am so bad tonight. Why I shall always be bad. Why I shall never act well again.

DORIAN. You made yourself ridiculous. My friends were bored; I was bored.

SYBIL. (*takes his hands*) My darling, before I knew you, acting was the one reality of my life. It was only in the theatre that I lived. I thought that it all was true. The joys of Beatrice were my joys, and the sorrows of Cordelia. I believed in everything. Then you came—oh, my beautiful love—and freed my soul from prison. Tonight, for the first time, I saw through all the shallowness, the sham, the silliness of the empty pageant in which I had always played. You have made me understand what life—what love—really is. You are more to me than art can ever be.

DORIAN. (*pulls his hands free, takes a backstep from her*) You have killed my love. You used to stir my imagination. Now you don't even stir my curiosity. I loved you because you gave shape and substance to the shadows of great art. You have thrown it all away. You are shallow and stupid. You are nothing to me now. I will never see you again. I will never mention your name. How can you say love mars your art! Without art you are nothing. You could have borne my name, been famous, had the world at your feet. What are you now? A third-rate actress with a pretty face.

SYBIL. (*almost paralyzed with shock*) You are not serious? You are acting—you are teasing—

DORIAN. (*mockingly*) I leave acting to you. You do it so well.

(*she reaches for him, but he pulls away*)
Don't touch me!

SYBIL. Don't leave me—please—don't leave me—!

(*MUSIC intros, and she sings:*)
My Prince Charming!
Your love superseded my art!
My world wasn't true,
And when I met you,
The real world encompassed my heart—!
Oh, Prince Charming,
The theatre's finished for me.
I can't play a role
When you fill my soul
With all that true living can be!
    DORIAN. All I understand is that you're boring me!
    SYBIL. Darling, take my hand—I love you, can't you
see—?
    DORIAN. Don't touch me. We're finished. I cannot
remain!
    SYBIL. Please don't go! Oh, darling! I can't bear the
pain!
(DORIAN *turns from her, exits from room, then from
    stage, via corridor, as she stands numbly,
    finishing:*)
My Prince Charming!
How briefly my heart was set free
By short moments of
His magical love,
A love that can nevermore be!
My life lies before me
In anguish and emptiness, for
My Prince Charming's no more!

(*Her voice breaks piteously on final words; then she
    stands there, much like someone with a violent
    head-injury who is totally dazed and cannot relate
    to her surroundings; as she remains there, im-
    mobile,* MRS. VANE *appears in corridor, with many
    bundles and bags, and moves happily into dressing-
    room*)

MRS. VANE. Oh, Sybil, wait till you *see* all the marvelous things I've bought. Now, for the wedding, I splurged on a hat you are going to adore—a nice, shiny black straw with a discreet red feather, and—and— (*reacts to* SYBIL's *appearance and silence*) Sybil— whatever is the matter with you—? I just saw your young man on his way out, and I thought—I thought—

SYBIL. (*manages to focus on events*) He's gone. He's abandoned me. He said I was shallow and stupid. There isn't going to be a wedding.

MRS. VANE. (*her face caves in, and she seems to shrivel*) No wedding. No wedding. Oh, the cruelty of it. The heartless beast.

(SYBIL *starts for her, arms outstretched for comfort*) How could he *do* such a thing to me?!

(*on the final word,* SYBIL *stops as if she'd run into a wall and her hands drop to her sides, as her mother slowly moves off with her bundles into the room beyond, during:*) What a thing to do to a poor old woman. He must have a heart of ice.

(*As* SYBIL *stands there, now with nowhere to turn for solace, the* STAGE MANAGER *comes down corridor and leans in door*)

STAGE MANAGER. 'Ere, now, wot's all this? Y'r supposed to be on the ruddy stage, y' young fool! Get a move on, now! It's the tomb scene, and the customers'll be howlin' for their money back if they don't see you kill yourself out there! Snap it up, lass!

SYBIL. (*slowly moves toward doorway*) Yes. We can't . . . disappoint the customers . . .

(LIGHTS FADE - end of scene)

SCENE 6

A London street (accomplished simply by having a tall streetlight, the gas-jet style, slide onstage near the proscenium, the only thing visible against the darkness). Raucous Music—such as introduces a shabby vaudeville act—begins immediately, and DORIAN *enters, strolling and swinging his cane quite jauntily, turns, smiles our way, tilts his hat rakishly to one side with the knob of his cane, then leans upon the cane, facing us. As soon as the raucous intro is completed, he will start to sing, but the instant he does so, there will appear a bit farther upstage (on the side opposite where he is posing beneath the streetlight) that pitiful stage again, the dropcloth up, and* SYBIL *standing there in her Juliet costume, holding Romeo's dagger (if you want to authenticize the tableau, you can also have "dead Romeo" lying beside her on the floor, clutching his emptied poison-vial, but this is not absolutely necessary). Intro ends, and:*

DORIAN. (*singing simultaneously with*) SYBIL

It was the only thing to do!	I have killed his love!
What other course could I pursue?	His parting words are more
Once I beheld her as she truly was,	Than flesh and blood can bear!
I had no other avenue!	
It was the only thing to do!	And the mem'ry of
When her attractiveness withdrew,	His heartless exit from my life
I nearly had a fit,	Has filled my soul with despair!

Finding her inadequate
To become the bride of a
    man whose
High position suits her
    not!
So I politely took my
    leave,
Removed her fingers from
    my sleeve,
And terminated that
Mournful interview!
The crushed heart soon
    recovers
When lovers prove
    untrue!
Her silly sentimental
    plan
Was far more
    transcendental than
The only thing a
    gentleman
Could do!

   (*He struts jauntily off,
his cane a-twirl, as* SYBIL
finishes:)

And all because I was
    unchained
By his love from the
    fantasies of
My former life.

All those foolishly
    fulfilling
Fancies which had
    fondly framed
My former life! He's set
    me free.
I'll not be wife to such
    as he.
If this be so, why should
    I be—
(*stabs herself*)
At all?

Now . .
Truly have I killed . . .
His . . .
Love . . .

(*and as he struts offstage and she falls and dies and
    raucous Music romps imperviously to its gaudy
    end—*)

(LIGHTS FADE - end of scene)

SCENE 7

The parlor of DORIAN'S *house. [NOTE: This is a bi-level set, with the attic room directly overhead, access to which is a railed spiral staircase downstage right, but the upper level is presently in gloom.] There can be many accouterments here, but the necessary ones are a writing-desk and chair, two wide and tall windows comprising most of the upstage wall, and the wide doorway, also downstage right, leading into the room. The portrait is also there, upstage, between the two windows; it has not yet been hung, and just stands there, leaning against the wall; the drapes of the window are drawn, and the room is in enough gloom so that we cannot see anything of the portrait but its lower half, clearly. Near the writing-desk is a tall, ornate folding-screen. There is a hurricane lamp upon the writing-desk. [In subsequent scenes when we do see the attic room, it will contain a window directly over the upstage right rear window of the parlor, the sort with door-like panes that open outward, plus a small schoolboy-size desk-and-chair, and a trunk of old clothing, curtains, draperies and such.] A moment after the Lights Come Up,* DORIAN *enters through door to hall [the door downstage right], weary but in a pleasant mood, and crosses the room to place his hat and cane on the desk. He stretches, yawns, glances about contentedly, and then looks toward the portrait and smiles.*

DORIAN. Ah, I'd almost forgotten about you, my beloved alter-ego. (*moves toward portrait*) So much has happened since Basil completed you yesterday—no, it's the day before that—it's nearly dawn, now. I feel much older and wiser than I did that day. I'm glad Basil could capture my youth when he had the chance. Here, now, you don't belong in gloom. . .

(*He moves to gas-tab beside the door, twists it, and the room-lights come up to half brightness—and we see that the portrait has changed—only slightly, but noticeably; the position of the head has altered a bit—from its noble stare off into space, it has now shifted to a stare right out at the beholder, and the mouth is twisted in a cynical smirk;* DORIAN *has not seen this as he re-approaches it*)

All right, now, refresh me—remind me of the handsome youth I am, and brush the cobwebs of disappointment and frustration from my aspect—(*sees the change; freezes in disbelief*) How—how extraordinary—it almost looks as if—No, it's a trick of the light. My eyes are weary from walking the foggy streets . . .

(*rushes back to tab and twists it; room brightens further*)

Now, then, we'll see what—(*stops, seeing that the change is really there*) It can't be! Such things do not happen in a sane world! It stares at me almost as if—as if it knew all about what happened at the theatre last night—as if—as if— (*starts in panic as he hears:*)

THOMAS. (*off*) Master Dorian? Is that you, sir—?

DORIAN. (*galvanized, looks frantically about, sees screen, rushes to it and brings it before portrait, then unfolds it to block the awesome alteration from view, during:*) He mustn't see it. None of the servants must see it. Unless . . . I've been out for many hours—could he *already* have seen it?

(*as he stands there in horrible uncertainty,* THOMAS, *his manservant, enters at door and stops*)

THOMAS. Oh, it *is* you, sir. You are risen early.

DORIAN. (*trying to be calm*) I—haven't been to bed. I've only just gotten home. Did—anything unusual happen in my absence?

THOMAS. No, sir. There have been no callers, no messages. Shall I open the drapes?

DORIAN. The drapes?

THOMAS. It's just coming on dawn, sir. You won't need these lights.

DORIAN. Oh, very well, very well!

(*Moves agitatedly to writing-desk, sits there, his back to the room, but we can see by his face that he is monitoring and sensing all of* THOMAS'S *movements as he opens the drapes nearest the door, passes the screen, then opens the other pair of drapes nearer* DORIAN. *Dawn light is indeed coming up brightly outside, and* THOMAS *then moves to the tab by the door and turns off the gas-lights. [DAWN LIGHT will come up brightly within the next fifteen seconds.]* THOMAS *looks about, then frowns at the sight of the screen and moves toward it. As he does so, MUSIC intros, and just as he reaches it,* DORIAN *spins to face him, still seated, and:*)

DORIAN. (*sings*) Well?

THOMAS.
I beg your pardon, sir, but I—

DORIAN.
What?

THOMAS.
I thought—

DORIAN.
Yes, what did you think?

THOMAS.
That the screen there in front of the portrait should be—

DORIAN.
Should be what?
THOMAS.
Moved aside, sir.
DORIAN.
Moved aside?!
THOMAS.
Aside.
DORIAN.
Don't you dare!
THOMAS.
But it's in the wrong place—
DORIAN.
Nonetheless, it remains!
THOMAS.
As you wish, sir.
DORIAN.
I do!
THOMAS. (*gestures toward screen, almost touching it*)
But I merely thought—
DORIAN. (*comes to his feet*)
Stop!
THOMAS. (*drops hand*)
Yes, of course, sir.
DORIAN.
Leave it alone!
        (*turns away, drops into chair, frightened*)
Did he see? Does he know?
Does he even suspect that the portrait is covered
Because I detected a change of expression that
Fills me with hideous fear?
If so, the man must go!
When he came in the room, there was something about
His demeanor that conjured a terrible doubt
In my mind, an impression that he may be masking a
    sneer!

THOMAS.
Will there be anything else, sir?
DORIAN. (*twists about on chair to face him*)
What?!
THOMAS.
I said—
DORIAN.
I heard what you said!
THOMAS.
Master Dorian, sir, is there anything wrong?
DORIAN.
Such as what?
THOMAS.
Sir, I only—
DORIAN. (*leaps to his feet*)
You're discharged!
THOMAS. (*startled*)
But, sir—?
DORIAN. (*advancing upon him*)
You are sacked!
THOMAS.
If I've done something wrong—?
DORIAN.
Will you go and get packed?!
THOMAS. (*bows, starts backing from room*)
As you wish, sir.
DORIAN.
Begone!
THOMAS. (*pauses in doorway*)
I am sorry if—
DORIAN. (*a roar of rage*)
Now!
THOMAS. (*exits on:*)
Very well, sir.
DORIAN. (*a final cry that propels* THOMAS *out of sight*)

Will you get out!
  (*shuts door, leans his back against it, trembling*)
Now I'm sure that he saw
That egregious flaw
In the face of the painting,
That odious tainting
Of beauty adorable twisted in horrible fright,
A blight upon my sight!
Well, he's gone, and good riddance,
But now must be hidden somewhere what my evil has
  wrought,
Where no other shall see the malignancy caught
On the canvas in glee . . .
That mold upon my soul,
That evil demon thing I seem to be,
That grinning stain of sin . . .
Of me!

(*Abruptly thrusts himself from door, rushes to desk,
  grabs up pen and paper as he sits, and begins
  writing frantically; while he is thus engaged, a very
  subdued* HENRY *enters from hall, hat in hand, his
  expression quite somber*)

HENRY. My dear boy—
      (DORIAN *turns, startled*)
I am so sorry for it all, Dorian, But you must not think
too much about it.
  DORIAN. Do you mean about Sybil Vane?
  HENRY. (*moving toward him, concerned*) Yes, of
course. It is dreadful, from one point of view, but it is
not your fault. Tell me, did you have a scene with her?
  DORIAN. I was brutal, Harry—perfectly brutal.
  HENRY. But you must not plunge yourself into
remorse over the matter.
  DORIAN. I have already passed through that phase. I
know you sneer at the idea of conscience, Harry, but it

does exist. I want to be good. I cannot bear the thought of my soul being hideous.

HENRY. That is certainly unique in my experience—an artistic basis for ethics. I congratulate you on it! But how do you intend to begin?

DORIAN. By marrying Sybil Vane.

HENRY. (*thunderstruck*) Marrying . . . Sybil Vane—?!

DORIAN. (*rises from chair, indicates pen and paper on desk*) I have been pouring my heart out to her, with wild words of sorrow and wilder words of pain. There is a luxury in self-reproach. When we blame ourselves we feel no one else has the right to blame us.

HENRY. But my dear Dorian—!

DORIAN. Now please, don't say something dreadful about marriage. You cut life to pieces with your epigrams.

HENRY. (*slowly realizing*) Then—you do not know, do you! When I heard, I came right over, not sure what would be a decent hour to waken you and tell you, but—when I saw your lights, I assumed. . .

DORIAN. Assumed what, Harry? What are you trying to tell me?

HENRY. Dorian—Sybil Vane is dead.

DORIAN. (*stares at him; then:*) Dead? Harry, what are you saying? Dead? When? How?

HENRY. The final act of the play. The tomb scene. When it came the moment for Juliet to impale herself upon Romeo's dagger . . . well . . . it was most certainly an enviable end for an actress—an inimitable performance.

DORIAN. Harry, this is terrible news. I cannot bear it. There can be no mistake about it?

HENRY. None. What is done is done. A fact is a fact. It cannot be altered.

DORIAN. (*looks toward the screen concealing the portrait*) Altered. Cannot be altered. (*moves toward screen, dazed, stands staring at it a moment, then straightens in a quivering rage*) She had no right to kill herself! It was wicked of her! How could she do such a thing to me!

HENRY. (*shocked*) Dorian!

DORIAN. You do not understand—what she has done to me—to my life . . .

HENRY. I understand only too well. And I must tell you that your marriage to her would have done you even worse. It was socially impossible. The whole thing would have been an absolute failure. Your good intentions toward her were pure vanity on your part. But I can see you are upset. I will make your apologies to Alan Campbell tonight at Lady Margaret's.

DORIAN. My apologies?

HENRY. He was most insistent that you come. He will wonder when you do not.

DORIAN. But Henry—I fully intend to be there.

HENRY. Tonight? At a party? After what has happened?

DORIAN. What better place to put the matter out of my mind. As you said—what is done is done. The thing cannot be altered. (*cannot forbear a brief glance toward the screen*) Harry, would you let yourself out? I have certain matters to attend to which may occupy the greater part of the morning.

HENRY. (*moving uncertainly toward door*) Yes, Dorian, certainly. But are you absolutely sure—?

DORIAN. I will see you at the party tonight.

HENRY. (*pauses in doorway*) Oh. There will probably be an official inquest into her death—I have no notion why—there is certainly no mystery to the matter—everyone at that performance saw what occurred. But if you should require the name of a good solicitor—

DORIAN. What has the inquest to do with me? No one there—not even Sybil—knew my right name. I have no wish to attend the inquest. What is done is done.

HENRY. As you say, Dorian. Well, then—I shall call for you tonight. (*exits*)

DORIAN. (*waits until the door closes, then removes screen and looks at altered portrait again*) I must hide you, you know. My old attic schoolroom should be just the place, with its stout door and my possession of the only key. If all my remorse and good intentions about Sybil have not changed you back—then so be it. You shall be my daily diary—the visible report on the condition of my soul. It may prove to be a fascinating relationship . . . (*and as he stands there staring at the portrait—*)

(*LIGHTS FADE - end of scene*)

SCENE 8

The ballroom of LADY MARGARET'S *house.* ALAN, BASIL, LADIES BEECHMONT *and* ELLERTON, *and* LORD BOYCE *are there, along with* LADY MARGARET *herself, all dressed in their best evening finery, standing about in various groups and chatting.* BASIL *is deep in conversation with* ALAN.

ALAN. But why are you so certain he will not come, Basil?

BASIL. There are things—private things—in his life which preclude it, I am afraid. I went round to his house this morning to commisserate with him, but was informed that he was indisposed and not seeing anybody today. I quite understood, of course.

ALAN. Well, I don't understand a bit of it. Can you tell me no more than you already have?

BASIL. I have no right. Should Dorian choose to tell you—that is another matter entirely.

(*there are two accesses to the ballroom—a large archway downstage right which comes from the house itself, and french doors, open, in the upstage wall, left, leading to the garden;* BASIL *now glances past* ALAN *to the former*)

Ah, but here is your charming fiancee, Alan.

(ALAN *looks that way as* GWEN *enters; she is a radiant beauty with coils of rich auburn hair, expensively gowned*)

ALAN. (*waves lightly toward her as she approaches, but says to* BASIL:) You must not call her that just yet—her family has a horror of jumping the gun on protocol. After the official announcement tonight—well—that is another matter.

(*moves to meet her as she draws near*)

Gwen, my darling! How simply marvelous you look!

GWEN. (*petulantly allows him to kiss her cheek*) But my entrance was spoiled, I fear. A woman should always enter a ballroom while music is playing. It gives a certain lovely lilt to her step. Why has the dancing not yet begun?

ALAN. (*as* BASIL *moves to join them*) Your mother, Lady Margaret, wished to await the arrival of the last guests, Lord Henry Wotton and Dorian Gray. But Basil tells me that Dorian may not be coming, after all—however, as to what's keeping Lord Henry—

GWEN. (*interrupts*) Dorian Gray? Not coming? But he is the most eligible bachelor in all of London! I wore this gown especially to impress him!

ALAN. Darling, what are you saying? Have you forgotten what we are to announce, tonight?

GWEN. Alan, our engagement is not official until Mother announces it. In the interim, I am still a young and beautiful and available young lady, and I had intended to enjoy my final moments of freedom toying with his heart.

BASIL. I fear you would have picked a bad moment for it, regardless, dear lady.

ALAN. That is right. I had forgotten. Dear Gwen, Dorian tells me he is quite enamored of some young lady already—(*belatedly frowns, looks toward* BASIL) Would have? Regardless? I don't follow that, Basil.

BASIL. (*retreating into his shell*) I beg your leave not to clarify my meaning. I said more than I should have, I fear.

GWEN. Ah, a mystery! Now I want more than ever to meet this Dorian Gray. I understand he is not only handsome, but wealthy as well.

ALAN. Gwen, my darling, when my medical studies have been completed—

GWEN. Yes-yes, Alan, we have been all over that. But until such time as you are a certified physician with a rich London practice, is it any wonder I am drawn to dream of men who have already found their place in society?

BASIL. (*uncertainly*) You *are* merely teasing this poor lad, I hope?

GWEN. (*laughs, and drops some of her petulant attitude*) Oh, of course I am, Basil. But Alan is so very easy to discomfit—I do confess I find a wicked sort of joy in doing so.

ALAN. (*much relieved*) Well, at any rate, you shan't have the opportunity tonight, for Dorian is not coming.

(BUTLER *appears in archway*)

BUTLER. Lord Henry Wotton, and the Honorable Mister Dorian Gray!

(ALL *in room turn to look as* HENRY *and* DORIAN *enter, and* BUTLER *exits*)

BASIL. Dorian . . . I can't believe it! How does he find the courage?

GWEN. More mysteries? This grows better and better. (*moves away from duo, heading directly for* DORIAN, *who is just in the process of greeting* LADY MARGARET)

DORIAN. It was so nice of you to allow me to come, at Alan's behest.

MARGARET. I am delighted you could, Mister Gray. We have heard so much about you!

GWEN. (*joining them*) But nowhere near enough!

MARGARET. Oh. Mister Dorian Gray—my daughter Gwen. Gwen, I believe you already know Lord Henry?

HENRY. We have had that good fortune, yes. Ah, there is Basil! Will you excuse me?

MARGARET. Now-now, you shall not escape my clutches so easily, Lord Henry! (*links arms with him*) We shall join your friend together. You possess the most wicked tongue in all of London, and I do not intend to miss a word you say tonight!

HENRY. (*as they go off toward* BASIL) Of that I have no doubt. Whether you will *understand* what I say is quite another matter!

(*she laughs, delighted, and they leave* DORIAN *and* GWEN *alone*)

DORIAN. You *are* delightful. Alan is a fortunate young man.

GWEN. And you are all I had hoped you would be, and more! But where is your young lady? Alan gave me to understand that you might bring her.

DORIAN. She is—indisposed, I fear. If my thirst for beauty becomes too acute, I may have to spend the greater part of the evening with *you.*

GWEN. Why, Mister Gray! What would Alan think!

DORIAN. Are you so sure Alan *does* think?

GWEN. Why—what an extraordinary thing to say!

DORIAN. I asked a question. You are postponing your answer.

(*MUSIC starts; it is a light, pleasant waltz*) Ah. Just the thing! That is what you require for total perfection—music. A girl such as you should be set to music.

GWEN. I—I should really have the first dance with Alan.

DORIAN. (*extends his arms to her*) Yes, you certainly should.

GWEN. He is coming this way!

DORIAN. He cannot object if we two should dance, can he? After all, where is the impropriety in a harmless waltz?

(*just as* ALAN *reaches them,* DORIAN *takes her into his arms, and they waltz away from him; he stands there, embarrassed and confused, as other couples—* MARGARET *and* HENRY, BASIL *and* ELLERTON, *and* BOYCE *and* BEECHMONT—*also begin to dance; the music remains pleasant, at first—but then—Lights Dim on* COUPLES, *until they are only vaguely seen in the shadows surrounding* DORIAN *and* GWEN, *and the MUSIC TURNS STRANGE, sensuous, increasing in tempo until it is veritably demonic;* DORIAN *retains his polite smile, but* GWEN's *face slowly grows entranced—almost frightened—as she looks up at him; then, at the climax of the music,* DORIAN *whirls her out through the french doors toward the garden, and—*)

[*BALLROOM SET and* OTHER COUPLES *slide off into the wings, and GARDEN SETTING— flowers, laden boughs, an arbor with a bench— moves downstage to create:*]

SCENE 9

Lady Margaret's garden. Music ceases precisely as the set comes into place. DORIAN *retains his embrace of* GWEN *as they stand before the bench.*

GWEN. We should not be out here. We must go back.

DORIAN. You have but to push my arms away, and you are free.

GWEN. What do you want of me?

DORIAN. What does any man want of a beautiful woman, in a lovely garden, on such an exquisite night?

GWEN. Sir, you overstep yourself. I have heard of men such as you.

DORIAN. And what have you heard?

GWEN. Nothing a lady would ever repeat!

DORIAN. (*amused*) Just listen to?

GWEN. What?!

DORIAN. Don't pretend to be shocked. Even fine young ladies must have some acquaintance with the darker side of human nature.

GWEN. (*pulls from his embrace, but does not move away*) I must say—you are certainly frank.

DORIAN. Subtlety is so time-consuming; there is nothing like candor for getting to the point. (*looks about*) This is such a lovely place. A man and woman might be tempted to do most anything in such a setting.

GWEN. I am going back into the house.

DORIAN. Am I preventing you?

GWEN. No, but—but—

DORIAN. (*embraces her; she does not respond, but does not resist*) From the moment I stepped into that room, and you came across the floor toward me—I knew that you were the loveliest creature I had ever seen. Words bubbled up inside me—words that I have never said to another woman—words that ached and pounded to be let free . . .

GWEN. Say them. Oh, Dorian—say them!
(*MUSIC intros, and:*)
DORIAN. (*sings*)
Your eyes, like candles in the mist . . .
Give rise to feeling too appealing to resist!
Are you the sweet conclusion of my quest?
You are so diff'rent . . . so diff'rent from the rest!
Your arms, whose promise of embrace
Alarms my heart as fingers start to interlace!
Enfold me, then, and hold me to your breast . . .
You are do diff'rent . . . so diff'rent from the rest!
(*her arms go about him, her gaze enraptured*)
BOTH.
My dream of ecstasy I now realize!
I seem at last to be held fast in paradise . . . !
DORIAN.
Your kiss . . . Oh, answer my appeal
For this sweet pleasure! Who can measure what I feel?
BOTH.
This longing may be wrong, but dare I leave it
   unexpressed . . .
To one so diff'rent . . . so diff'rent from the rest . . . ?!

(*they sink down together upon the bench, and kiss,
   ardently, hungrily, as—*)

(LIGHTS FADE - end of scene)

SCENE 10

Though the scene is DORIAN'S *parlor/attic, all we see is
the portrait; it is now in the attic, against the back
wall beside the door-hinged double-window. During the course of the musical number that opens*

this scene, the portrait will change before our eyes [see SPECIAL EFFECTS]: The face will contort into that of a fiend, the back will hunch, the figure stoop slightly, the fingers gnarl like claws, the clothing will tatter and wrinkle and soil—but the flowers and such behind the figure in the painting will remain incongruously fresh as ever, making the figure the more hideous by contrast. The moment the scene begins, we hear MUSIC intro, and:

UNSEEN CHORUS. (*sings*)
And so it went for twenty years, for handsome Dorian
  Gray:
A dilly here, a dally there, and never aging a day!
  MALE VOICES.
He never aged a day!
  ALL VOICES.
His sins grew more than scarlet, they were blacker than
  the Pit,
And still he searched afar for darker deeds he might
  commit!
His hunger for sensation was a force beyond control . . .
And then he would return to read the record of his soul
  . . .

(*Lights Come Up on attic room;* DORIAN *is seated in chair, staring at the portrait;* MUSIC *has blended from end of CHORUS-number into beginning of new song, and—*)

  DORIAN. (*sings quietly, somberly*)
Something new . . . There's always something new . . .
A dusting of depravity . . . or soft decay . . .
To greet me each new day as I scan the canvas
Here in fearful view . . .
        (*picks up hand-mirror from desk, rises*)
Then I stand with a mirror in my trembling hand,
And I peer into the glass . . . only to see

A youthful face, and I sigh in relief
As the curtaining cloth—
(*moves large velvet shroud-like cloth which is secured at
     upper left corner of painting across the portrait*)
Upon the fiend I replace . . .
     (*has cloth secured, turns his back upon portrait*)
Then I do anything I'm longing to . . .
Till the dawn when I renew
(*moves his head slightly, looking back toward portrait*)
The crumbling view of something new . . . !

(*He stands, wearily, as MUSIC finishes, then looks up as
     VICTOR, his new manservant, enters below and
     moves to foot of stairs and calls up:*)

VICTOR. Master Dorian, sir—? You asked me to remind you when it was time to depart for Lady Beechmont's . . .

DORIAN. Is it so late already?! (*will start downstairs*)

VICTOR. Yes, sir, it is. Do you have your cigar-
ettes—your wallet—?

DORIAN. Yes, yes, I have everything—though I'm not
entirely certain I really wish to go.

VICTOR. Not go, sir? Are you feeling unwell?

DORIAN. Let us say that I—am weary, Victor. I have
been attending these dinners for two decades, and I can
almost predict every dull and tiresome thing that will be
said and done there.

VICTOR. Two decades! If you'll pardon my saying so,
sir, you certainly don't seem old enough a man to have
done so. You could pass for a lad of twenty.

DORIAN. You're very kind to say so, Victor. I would
like to maintain that I owe it all to plenty of fresh air,
sound sleep and spotless living—but I am ill-acquainted
with any of them, I fear.

VICTOR. You are jesting, sir.

DORIAN. Yes. Yes, I suppose I am. But it's a very sad jest, Victor . . . a very sad jest, indeed . . .

(*he will exit toward hall,* VICTOR *staring after him*)

(LIGHTS FADE - end of scene)

SCENE 11

The dining room at Lady Beechmont's house. [See Scene 3] DORIAN *is not yet at table, but the others from the similar scene—with the natural exception of* ALAN—*are all there, the two ladies now being in opposite places to where they sat earlier. There is a newcomer in the chair formerly occupied by* ALAN—*her name is* HETTY, *and she is possibly the most radiantly beautiful blonde woman on the face of the earth—fresh, young and vivacious.* OTHERS *have all grayed and aged.*

HETTY. I do wonder what is keeping your friend Mister Gray. I have so been looking forward to meeting him, Harry.

HENRY. And Dorian has a rare treat in store, himself, when he sets his eyes upon *you,* my dear.

ELLERTON. Oh, Hetty, you mustn't pry into Dorian's affairs. He has the most scandalous reputation!

BOYCE. There are certain gentlemen who pointedly get up and leave the room when he enters, nowadays.

BEECHMONT. And ladies who blush quite crimson and avoid his eye!

BASIL. Gossip! Filthy gossip! Why, one has but to *look* upon the lad to see there cannot be a particle of truth to such tales. Mark my words, they are born of envy at his remarkable good looks and general aspect.

HETTY. Of course, they do say that where there's smoke—

HENRY. (*completing her phrase*)—there is Lady Beechmont's kitchen.

BEECHMONT. (*laughs*) Harry, you are are such an asset to my parties. You always know the wrong thing to say. Hetty, my dear, if you would like to move to another place, farther away from him, I will quite understand.

HETTY. But I find him completely charming, Lady Beechmont.

HENRY. I never argue with a beautiful lady.

BOYCE. Yes, but seriously, what *of* Dorian Gray? I have heard the most dreadful tales about him—

ELLERTON. Yes, they do say that he—

BASIL. *Who* say?!

ELLERTON. Why—everyone. You know—people in general.

BASIL. Well, I for one, refuse to listen to any such sordid scandalmongering!

BEECHMONT. Oh, but Basil, you deprive yourself of the juiciest tales ever to circulate in polite society!

HETTY. Precisely what *do* they day about him?
(MUSIC intros)

QUARTET. (*only* HETTY *and* BASIL *not singing*)
They say in the light of day
He is all a gentleman could be.
To his reputation they'd never raise a doubt.
And yet, when the sun has set,
Ev'rything is not as it should be:
A strange, unbecoming change seems to come about!
A queer metamorphosis alters his mood,
That's hard to ignore as his manners turn crude,
And weekends his habit is wand'ring afar
To frequent establishments oddly bizarre!
They say, when he has his way,

Though we can't remember who said it,
A lady is soon persuaded to go astray!
But when we see him again,
We are very hard put to credit
A piece of it, but at least, that is what they say!
Though we hope and pray it is mere hearsay,
Yet it truly may be that Dorian Gray
Often goes astray! He should feel dismay,
But he does it day after day anyway . . .
So they say!

BASIL. Outrageous! You have only to look at the young man, Hetty, and—

HENRY. She shall have her chance—for here he comes, now!

(ALL *look up as* DORIAN *hastens into the room*)

DORIAN. (*taking his place at the table*) A thousand apologies, Lady Beechmont. I lost track of the time!

BASIL. You have missed a most excellent clam broth.

HENRY. I rather suspect the clam may have missed it, as well.

HETTY. Harry, don't! Why, you spooned it down so fast and furiously, your bowl probably needn't even be washed!

(OTHERS *laugh*)

DORIAN. (*focusing for the first time on the source of the comment*) I don't believe I have had the pleasure—? (*rises from his place*)

HENRY. Then it's the only one you haven't had, to hear these others talk. Dorian Gray—Hetty Duval.

DORIAN. I am charmed.

HETTY. You are charming.

DORIAN. I stand corrected.

HETTY. But please do sit back down.

DORIAN. (*still on his feet*) Harry, would I be rude if I asked you to exchange places with me?

HENRY. Exceedingly. But I should be ruder to refuse you.

(*Rises, allows* DORIAN *to sit beside* HETTY, *takes* DORIAN's *vacated place, during:*)

HETTY. Harry has told me that you are a man his own age. Seeing you, I find that difficult to believe.

DORIAN. Perhaps I dye my hair.

HETTY. And how do you account for your flawless face?

DORIAN. I do not account for it. I simply endure it. What is mine is mine. I take no credit.

HETTY. Do you know, I was expecting someone of quite different aspect—I rather thought you would be wizened up with the onus of unspeakable sins and desperate vice.

DORIAN. Perhaps I am, and the light in the room is merely too dim to show it.

HETTY. No more of that. You are quite the handsomest man I have ever met.

DORIAN. And you the loveliest lady.

HETTY. You toy with me.

DORIAN. Is that a commentary or a recommendation?

BASIL. Really, Dorian—you forget yourself!

DORIAN. Looking upon Hetty's face, how could I think of anything but her beauty?

HETTY. I don't mind, Basil. His candor is most refreshing.

BASIL. His import is scandalous. Dorian—I have been defending you to these people—perhaps I have been in error. (*rises*) If you will excuse me, Lady Beechmont, the hour grows late, and I have to catch the boat-train in less than an hour.

HENRY. You are going abroad, Basil?

BASIL. My customary jaunt to warmer climes as winter draws near. There is nothing so inspiring as the South of France to an artist this time of year. (*glances toward* DORIAN) There *was* something more inspiring to me—once—but now—I wonder—

BEECHMONT. Basil, I forgive your early departure. You shall miss your train.

BASIL. Yes, you are quite right. I must go. I shall see you all again, of course, come spring. (*exits from room*)

HENRY. A shame he shall miss the always-excellent desserts with which you cap off these feasts, Lady Beechmont. Might I have his portion?

BEECHMONT. Harry, that would be bad for your gout.

HENRY. I don't see why I should do anything *good* for my gout, do you?

(OTHERS *laugh*)

HETTY. Your friends are very amusing, Mister Gray.

DORIAN. "Dorian," please. And they may be amusing to you, but believe me, I have heard every one of their aphorisms a hundred times, and they begin to pall on my sensitivities.

HETTY. You don't mean that.

DORIAN. Ah, would that I did not. I tell you, dear lady, I have dined with this same group for the past twenty years, now, and the conversation is so similar on each occasion that it might be etched in stone!

HETTY. Are they really so bad as that?

DORIAN. Just listen for yourself!

(*MUSIC intros, and:*)

BOYCE. (*sings*)
Parliament will be in session in a week or two—
BEECHMONT.
Discussing Lady Bentley's indiscretion off in Timbuktu.

BOYCE.
I hear the new prime minister
Has promised that within his term
Of office nothing sinister shall cause his Waterloo.
ELLERTON.
Friday I'll endure a tea at Lady Bligh's affair,
Collecting clothing for the poor and needy.
Will I see you there?
BEECHMONT.
I don't think I could bear a tea
Providing clothes for charity,
When I have nothing fit to wear!
ELLERTON.
This is so delicious!
Will you share the recipe?
(HENRY *opens his mouth and leans foward to comment, but:*)
DORIAN. (*to*   HENRY, *for* HETTY's *benefit—and she is amused*)
If she's referring to the fish,
You'd rather bury it at sea!
HENRY.
Why Dorian, that's most unkind!
DORIAN.
Oh, Harry, you don't really mind!
You're merely out of sorts to find I've got a memory!
BOYCE.
How do you suppose the pound will fare in foreign
trade
Now that the upper house is honor-bound to back a
French blockage?
ELLERTON.
Why babble of the balance-sheet,
As long as there's enough to eat?
DORIAN.
Her pounds can never be mislaid!

HENRY. (*still a bit ruffled at* DORIAN *stealing his thunder*)
Mocking people of our group
Ill-suits these nice affairs.
DORIAN.
But I am merely your devoted pupil,
Echoing your airs.
HENRY.
Why, Dorian, I'm truly shocked
To hear my social notions mocked!
DORIAN.
Oh, really, Harry, save your lamentations for your prayers!
(*to* HETTY)
Gentlemen's and ladies' speech is always indiscreet,
Since all they're good for is monotony
Too boring to repeat.
OTHERS. (*except* HETTY)
A dose of degradation puts a kick in conversation—
DORIAN.
But it's always done the same old way!
OTHERS. (*except* HETTY)
That's true of all we say and do!
We're punished, though, since we have to
Remember ev'ry word we say!
DORIAN. (*to* HETTY, *who is laughing at end of song*)
There's not a word of truth in that statement. They never hear a thing but the sound of their own voices.

HETTY. If you find them so intolerable, why do you attend these affairs?

DORIAN. (*half-turns away, growing melancholy*) They are—my friends. Whatever else they may be, they are my friends. I—do not have so many friends as I once had.

HETTY. *I* should like to be your friend, Dorian.

DORIAN. (*looks toward her, pauses, then says, with reborn enthusiasm*) I am having them down to my country place this coming weekend, for some hunting and general merriment. Will you come?

HETTY. I should enjoy that very much, Dorian. Yes, I will surely come.

DORIAN. You know—you *are* the loveliest creature I have ever met . . .

HETTY. You have said that to other women, though, have you not?

DORIAN. Yes, I have. But this is the first time I truly meant it . . .

(*He places his hand over her own, and they look into each others eyes, not speaking, as—*)

(LIGHTS FADE - end of scene)

SCENE 12

Dorian's house, parlor and attic, both shrouded in gloom, but slightly visible. After a moment, DORIAN enters lower room, whistling theme of "CONVERSATION" song, his manner happy and jaunty. He turns his back to the room to turn the tab that brings up LOWER ROOM LIGHTS, and we see that BASIL, in overcoat and hat, is seated in the chair at the writing-desk, but facing toward the doorway. DORIAN holds his own hat in one hand, his overcoat over the same arm, and as he turns and sees he is not alone, he drops them, on:

DORIAN. What—?! Oh, Basil, my friend, it's you! You gave me quite a start. (*will retrieve his fallen articles during:*)

BASIL. I didn't take the train after all. I sent my luggage on ahead, then came back here. (*comes to his feet*) Dorian, my dear friend—we must talk. We really must.

DORIAN. (*uneasy, not wanting to continue the topic*) How in the world did you get in? My manservant hates to be awakened at these late hours—that's why I never go out without my latchkey. He's quite imperious about it—and you know how hard good servants are to get, these days—and keep.

BASIL. Dorian, you are babbling. Please stop. There should be no illness-at-ease between two friends.

DORIAN. Which I hope we shall always be, Basil.

BASIL. (*moves to him, clasps his upper arms*) Oh, we will, Dorian, we will. I could not bear it not to see you.

DORIAN. Hush, keep your voice down. My manservant may not yet have gone back to sleep.

BASIL. Oh, no fear of that, Dorian. I did not wake him. I noticed from the street that your garden door was ajar. I let myself in. I hope you do not mind?

DORIAN. No, of course I don't. But this is not like you, Basil, sneaking into people's houses in the dead of night—

BASIL. Dorian, spare me your polite conversation. The last train to the boat leaves in less than half an hour, and I must be on it. Please—let us talk.

DORIAN. (*who needs one badly, and it shows*) Surely you have time for a brandy—? (*Moves to small sideboard, and pours out two glasses from a decanter, his back to* BASIL, *though we can see his face is creased with a worried frown of apprehension*) It's Napoleon. I have to keep it on hand in case Harry drops by. You know his appetite for the finer things in life—

BASIL. Dorian, stop! I must speak. I can contain myself no longer.

DORIAN. (*turns quietly, hands* BASIL *a brandy; then:*) Very well. Contain yourself no longer.

BASIL. Do not mock me, I pray you.

DORIAN. Now it is you who are babbling. If you have something to say, say it. (*angrily flings himself down on a chaise*) What is it all about? I hope it is not about myself. I am tired of myself tonight. I would rather be somebody else. Hetty and I quite exhausted me as a topic of conversation.

BASIL. But it is about you, Dorian. I think it right that you should know that the most dreadful things are being said against you in London.

DORIAN. I don't wish to know about them. I love scandals about other people, but scandals about myself don't interest me. They have not got the charm of novelty.

BASIL. They must interest you. Every gentleman is interested in his good name. You don't want people to tell of you as something vile and degraded. You have your wealth and position, but those are not everything. Mind you, I don't believe the rumors—not, at least, when I see you.

DORIAN. Then what a shame you are going away.

BASIL. Don't be flippant, Dorian, this is most dreadfully serious. Sin is a thing that writes itself across a man's face. It cannot be concealed. There are no such things as secret vices.

DORIAN. How can you possibly know that? A true secret vice would *not* show itself.

BASIL. Do not play at words with me. I have come to warn you. You, with your pure, bright, innocent face and your marvelous, untroubled youth—I can't believe anything against you. And yet—I have heard stories—terrible stories—from people who would have no reason to invent them. And why do so many of your friends end in degradation and despair? That poor boy in the guards who committed suicide—and Sir Henry Ashton, who had to leave England with a tarnished name—You and he were inseparable! What about Adrian Singleton, and his dreadful end? What about Lord Kent's only son, and his career? I met his father yesterday in Saint James Street. He seemed broken with shame and sorrow. What about the young Duke of Perth? What sort of life has he got now? What gentleman would associate with him?!

DORIAN. (*surges to his feet*) Stop, Basil! You—you talk of things about which you know nothing! If people depart the room when I enter it, it is because I know something of their vices, not they of mine! Did I teach Ashton his vices, and young Perth his debauchery? If Kent's silly son takes his wife from the streets what is that to me? If Adrian Singleton writes his friend's name across a bill, am I his keeper? What right have you to judge me?

BASIL. (*quietly*) One has the right to judge of a man by the effect he has over his friends. Yours seem to lose all sense of honor, of goodness, of purity. You have filled them with a madness for pleasure. They have gone down into the depths. You led them there. Yes—you led them there, and yet you can smile as you are smiling now. And did not your friendship for Harry prevent you from making his sister's name a byword?!

DORIAN. Take care, Basil. You go too far.

BASIL. And now that sweet young girl, Hetty Duval—!

(DORIAN *stiffens*)

I saw you with her tonight at dinner—heard the things you said—the things you intimated—it was a side of you I did not know existed—! It made me think that the rumors about that poor Gwen—Lady Margaret's daughter—might also be true. Can they be true? Dorian, I do not want to stand here and preach to you—

DORIAN. Harry says that every man who turns himself into an amateur curate for the moment always begins by saying that, and then proceeding to break his word.

BASIL. (*crushed by his levity*) I only want you to lead a life as will make you a man the world loves and respects. You have a wonderful influence on people. Let it be for good, not for evil. They say that you corrupt everyone with whom you become an intimate—I am told things that become impossible to doubt. Lord Gloucester showed me a letter his wife had written to him when she lay dying, alone, in her villa at Mentone. Your name was implicated in the most terrible confession I ever read. I told him it was absurd—that I knew you thoroughly—that you were incapable of such things—and yet—I wonder if I do know you ? Before I could answer that, I should have to see your very soul—!

DORIAN. (*takes brandy glass from* BASIL, *sets both glasses down*) Then you shall see it. This very night. (*turns up flame in hurricane lamp on desk, picks up lamp*) Come. It is your own handiwork. Why shouldn't you see it!

(*Followed by a bewildered* BASIL, *he moves from the room, lowering the parlor lights as he exits, and starts up the stairs,* BASIL *trailing after him*)
You can tell the world about it afterward, if you choose. Nobody would believe you.

BASIL. Dorian, what are you saying?

DORIAN. Come, I tell you. You have chattered enough about corruption. Now you shall look on it face to face.

BASIL. But where are we going? What is upstairs?

DORIAN. A diary of my life. But do not worry about your train. You shall not have to read long.

(*They are in attic, now, and* DORIAN *sets lamp on desk, and turns it up so that ATTIC BRIGHTENS; the cloth covers the face of the portrait from top to bottom, still)*

BASIL. What is this room? Why have you brought me here?

DORIAN. (*moves to portrait, takes hold of cloth*) You are the one man in the world who is entitled to know everything about me, Basil. You have had more to do with my life than you think. You think that only God can see the soul? I have but to draw this curtain back, and you shall see mine!

BASIL. Dorian, have you gone mad?!

DORIAN. I thought I had, the first time I viewed this monstrous thing, in its first contortion of depravity. But it is real. Horribly real. (*he pulls aside the cloth, and lets it drop to hang from the corner of the painting; the monster is as we last saw it before he went to dinner)*

BASIL. (*staggers back with a loud cry of horror*) Good lord! Dorian—what does this mean—what is this thing—this unspeakably foul thing? And—why does it look so terrifyingly familiar?

DORIAN. Because you painted it. Long ago. In a springtime garden filled with the scent of lilac. And I made a foolish, almost casual, wish . . .

BASIL. It is monstrous. You should destroy it.

DORIAN. (*turns away to stare wearily out window*) It has already destroyed me.

BASIL. And to think I thought it the best thing I had ever done . . . what sort of man have I worshiped? This has the face of a satyr—the eyes of a devil!

DORIAN. It is the face of my soul.

BASIL. (*turns away, his face contorted with revulsion, drops into chair at desk, stunned*) My God! If it is true—and this is what you have done with your life—why, you must be far worse, then, than those who talk against you fancy you to be! Oh, Dorian, what a lesson! What a terrible lesson it has taught you! And me! I worshiped you, and am now punished for it. You worshiped yourself, and are punished for it. Dorian, you must pray, pray for forgiveness. We must both pray, now, here, together!

DORIAN. It is too late, Basil.

(*MUSIC intros*)

BASIL. It cannot be. It must not be! (*clasps his hands, elbows upon the desk, raised his face upward, closes his eyes, and sings:*)
Come, kneel in devout supplication
And ask for His love.
For only through God can your soul be healed
May he be your shield, this we pray.

(DORIAN *slowly turns, looks toward him*)
And lead us not into temptation,
Dear Father above.
And grant us that we in Thy grace shall grow.
God of goodness, show us the way!

(DORIAN *moves forward, stands over him, his face twisted with contempt—with weariness—with despair*)
Your soul has been wounded by your sinful ways;
Your vanity and your pride.
But now put an end to all your sinful days,
And ask God to be your guide . . .

(DORIAN *turns away angrily; there is a small, sharp, fruit-knife lying on a dusty trunk; he picks it up, turns, moves toward* BASIL's *back, during:*)
Together we'll beg His forgiveness;
He'll answer our prayer.
So, my friend, join with me
In an earnest plea . . .
Only ask Him and He
Will be there . . .

(DORIAN, *trembling with uncontrollable fury, raises knife*)
Not a moment to spare, for—

(DORIAN *stabs* BASIL; BASIL *rises from the chair, which topples backward, with a shrill cry of agony;* DORIAN *stabs him again and again;* MUSIC *has paused at the stabbing; now* BASIL *topples and spawls across the desk;* DORIAN *just stands there, looking at him;* MUSIC *comes up again, and mournfully completes the interrupted melody, as* ALL LIGHT *but the* LIGHT UPON THE PICTURE *fades—and we see that its hands are now dripping with blood that lies in gory puddles at it feet*)

(LIGHTS FADE VERY SLOWLY - end of scene)

SCENE 13

Lights Come Up Slowly on Dorian's parlor. [We can see the attic room dimly; BASIL *still lies across the desk but the portrait has been re-covered.]* DORIAN *is at writing-desk, busy with pen and paper;* VICTOR *enters from hall.*

VICTOR. Master Dorian, sir? A Mister Alan Campbell is here to see you.
DORIAN. What? Oh, yes, Alan, of course. Show him in, Victor, show him in!

(VICTOR *opens door farther, and* ALAN *enters; he is older, of sterner face, and somehow stronger than when we last saw him; he stands just inside door until* VICTOR *exits*)

DORIAN. I shall be with you in a moment, Alan, as soon as I finish writing this. Have a seat—help yourself to some brandy. (*keeps writing*)

ALAN. (*remains where he is*) I only came because your note said it was a matter of life or death. I had intended never to enter your house again.

DORIAN. (*his back still turned to him, busily folding page and inserting it into an envelope*) Yes, it is a matter of life or death, Alan. I thank you for coming.

ALAN. Spare me your fine manners. I have never forgiven you for Gwen's death. I never shall. Lady Margaret is a broken woman, a veritable recluse, since that terrible tragedy. She owes her good fortune to you.

DORIAN. (*sealing envelope*) Now truly, Alan, am I to be blamed if that wretched girl happened to be on a boat which didn't quite make it across to France? (*stands and turns, envelope in hand*) How well you look. The years have been kind to you.

ALAN. Not so kind as they have been to you—I confess your appearance is incedible for a man your age . . . But that is neither here nor there. What do you want of me?

DORIAN. Merely a gesture of friendship, Alan. Are you sure you won't have that brandy?

ALAN. I only came here because, as a doctor, I felt bound to come to anyone who summoned me so desperately—even to you. But I see you are as well as ever, so—if you will excuse me—? (*turns to door*)

DORIAN. (*quietly*) I saw Gwen the other day.

ALAN. (*freezes, then turns slowly back*) You are mad.

DORIAN. Ah, would that I were, but no, it is a fact. It seems that the poor girl never did make it to that boat, after all. As the American author Mark Twain once so neatly put it, the reports of her death were greatly exaggerated.

ALAN. (*takes a step toward him, stops*) Gwen. Alive.

DORIAN. Oh, you shouldn't know her by sight. She has changed, Alan, changed for the worse, I fear. But alive, nevertheless.

ALAN. (*moving toward him*) But where is she—how is she—?!

DORIAN. Will you have that brandy now?

ALAN. Yes. I believe I will.

DORIAN. (*proceeds to pour two glassfuls*) It was down by the docks, a most wretched neighborhood, but whose grimy buildings contain peculiar delights for those who know where to look—oh, she did not see me, I made certain of that, but there was something in her profile that struck a responsive chord in my memory, and then I heard her speak, and knew her. Not that her voice is quite so imperious and charming, anymore—but there are certain things— a rhythm of speech, a habit of inflection—which never alter in a person. I followed her—at a discreet distance, you may be sure—

(*will now move with brandy to* ALAN, *who accepts a glass*)

to her place of lodging, and wrote down the address. In fact, I have just written down that very address in this letter which I intend to post immediately—unless, of course, you decide to wish after all to render me a small assistance?

ALAN. What letter? What are you saying? Let me see that! (*takes envelope from* DORIAN'*s hand, gasps, drops it*) Lady Margaret! You'd send such a thing to Lady Margaret? The knowledge would shatter her mind!

DORIAN. But think of the joy of a mother finding her long-lost child, Alan.

ALAN. You are a monster. I shan't lift a finger to help you.

DORIAN. Oh, but Alan, you simply must!

(MUSIC intros, and he sings:)
I have a task for you, my friend,
Whose execution can't be shoddy:
I beg you to consent to lend a hand
Disposing of a body.

(ALAN reacts)
My attic room is the temporary tomb
Of a gentleman I stabbed last night,
And surely you have the special talent to
Get his last remains completely out of sight.
His clothing and his flesh and bone
Must disappear, but don't you worry:
He only weighed eleven stone,
So he should vanish in a hurry.
(ALAN stares at him in wonderment, shaking his head)
By chemistry, you can do it, don't you see?
That is why your talent I command.
Some acid will likely do it, but don't spill,
For the carpet is quite new, you understand.

ALAN *(sardonically amused)*
You're mad, my friend, I must infer.
I must decline and beg your pardon.
As for your corpse, you'd best inter
His quaint cadaver in your garden.
Just dig a hole—work is tonic for the soul,
Though it may not help a man who kills.
Then plant him deep, do it quickly—he won't keep—
Plus it might do wonders for your daffodils!
*(sets down brandy, turns to go, but DORIAN lays a hand
on his arm and restrains him)*

DORIAN.
I've some advice for you, my friend,
A word of caution you should heed now:
There's still this letter I intend
To post should you not do this deed now!
(ALAN stops, trapped)

So do repair to the room above the stair,
And preserve dear Lady Marg'ret's mind.
                    (*rises brandy glass*)
Here's to success! But I pray, don't make a mess—
A good cleaning lady's very hard to find!
                    (*happily drains his glass*)
ALAN. I—I will do as you say. But—I must go and get some things—some chemicals—some equipment—

DORIAN. Go to that desk and write down everything you will require. My man will go round to your laboratory and fetch everything. You are to remain here until the job is completed, is that understood?

ALAN. (*nods, defeated*) Understood.

DORIAN. Splendid. I will go and summon my man at once. (*starts for door, retrieving fallen letter en route*)

ALAN. Dorian—

DORIAN. (*stops, turns*) Yes, Alan?

ALAN. Did you ever wonder *why* poor Gwen was taking that boat to France?

DORIAN. No. Oh, I heard vague rumors, of course—some sort of scandal or other that might be prevented from becoming public if she could flee the country for a bit.

ALAN. She was about to bear your child.

DORIAN. *My* . . . child . . . ? But—if she never sailed on that boat—what became of the child?!

ALAN. (*smiling; it is the only triumph he has*) We shall never know, now, shall we!
                    (*straightens as* DORIAN *crumples slightly*)
Ah, what a pleasure it is to see that smile leave your face for once. I used to wonder what terrible vengeance I might wreak upon you—now I believe I have achieved it.

(*and as the two men stand staring at one another—*)

(LIGHTS FADE - end of scene)

SCENE 14

*The downstairs room of an opium den near the docks.
A short portion of stairs leading up to the "smok-
ing rooms" can be seen at the rear; downstage left
is the door to the street; there is a grimy bar along
the right wall, with a sullen* BARTENDER *in back of
it, and a fireplace, with a soup-kettle hanging on
the hob over the fire, along the opposite wall, just
upstage of the door. Old* GWEN *and two* HAGS *are
leaning against the bar, each with a mug of beer.
Music intros, and—*

HAG –1. (*sings*)
Paris fashions fill good Queen Victoria with despair—
   GWEN.
Because she doesn't think the men would wink
At armpits full of hair!
   BARTENDER.
Prince Albert dines on bread and jam
While he's abed at Buckingham—
   GWEN.
And soils the royal monogram upon his underwear!
   HAG –2.
Royalty is apt to make a fuss when in a funk,
When all Prince Albert has to do
Is take her out and get her drunk!
   ALL.
Although it's rotten etiquette
Insulting folks we've never met,
It dulls the pain and we forget
How low we've sunk!
Deep in degradation, when we might demand a meth-
Od of our quick extermination, and our dearest dream
   is death,
We hasten here and in the dark-

Ened room above we strike a spark
And feel the sweet caress of narc-
Olepsis on our breath!
Though anyone's morale is low within this awful place,
One pipe'll turn it to a palace where we're wallowing in
    lace!
If we look sad and sloppy, do not blame the pretty
    poppy
For oblivion in pipes of clay:
When people lacking hope become acquaintances of
    opium,
Nirvana's just a puff away!

(*song over, they sigh and just sag there, wearily, and do
not even turn as street door opens and* DORIAN
*enters, in hat and Inverness cape, the collar turned
up to hide his face: he pauses, seems satisfied,
lowers collar, and moves toward bar, looks the
women over and recognizes* GWEN; *he goes to her,
takes her by the arm*)

DORIAN. Gwen! I must speak with you! It is most
urgent!

GWEN. (*looks him up and down beerily, without
recognition, pulls her arm free, and returns to leaning
on bar, on:*) Not tonight dearie, I have a headache!

DORIAN. Gwen! Gwen, don't you know me? It's
Dorian! (*she stiffens, then turns her head slowly his
way*) I must speak with you, now!

GWEN. (*straightens, stares at him, sobers con-
siderably*) By all that's unholy! It is you! Come a bit
late, ain't you, dearie? My dance-card's all filled!

DORIAN. (*Pulling her away from the bar, where*
HAGS *and* BARTENDER *have started to show an interest
in their conversation*) Gwen, you must listen to me—I
thought you were *dead*, until a short while ago! I only
just learned about the child! What became of it?

GWEN. (*befogged*) Child? What child? Oh, *that* bloody brat! How the hell do *I* know? That's a lifetime ago. Chopped up and made into sausage, for all I care. (*peers closely at him*) You know, it's crazy, but—you look the same age as the last time I saw you—or am I going mad?

DORIAN. Gwen, the child! What has become of it?

GWEN. I can't remember. It was so long ago. (*suddenly sly*) But a nice glass of whiskey might help my poor old memory a bit—

DORIAN. (*know he's being guyed, but tows her toward the bar*) Here, my man—(*tosses a coin on the bar*) Whiskey for the lady—all she wants—the whole bottle, if need be!

GWEN. (*as bartender finds a bottle and shotglass*) Well, now, better and better! "Lady," it is! How nice of you to notice! (*leans grotesquely close to him*) You wouldn't be wanting to have a bit o' fun, now, would you? Whiskey always makes my headaches go away, fast.

DORIAN. Don't be disgusting!

GWEN. (*cackles hoarsely*) Disgusting, is it! That's not the way you used to talk!

(*MUSIC intros, and she sings*)

What's the matter, cutie,
Lost your eye for beauty?
What a bloody shame!
Look into my eyes
And promise paradise again!
Used to be a time you
Couldn't live without me;
Ev'rything about me
Stirred your soul,
Or so you told me then!
A little bit of lust,
You told me then, was just

A game that lovers play,
But too late I found
You didn't play it by the rules!
By the time I knew the score,
I found you weren't playing any more!
Girls who play at love are
Most extraordinary fools!

(BARTENDER *now places bottle and glass upon bar*
before her, and as she starts pouring hungrily,
DORIAN *addresses him:*)

DORIAN.
Woman's memory is unrelenting, she must
Dwell upon the past,
Fanning embers of an antiquated love affair!
Don't they realize incessant resurrections
Of a dead affection's
Greater than a mortal man can bear!

GWEN. (*to* BARTENDER, *indicating* DORIAN *with a*
casual thumb)
Standing there before me,
Trying to ignore me,
Isn't he a scream!

(*to* DORIAN, *viciously*)
Feeding on a fallen
Woman's tears is all you know!
If you offered me romance,
I wouldn't take another bloody chance!
So, Prince Charming, pack up all your fancy airs, and
  go!

(*hurls dregs of her drink into his face; he lurches back,*
wiping at his eyes, his back turned toward stairs, as
JAMES VANE—*older now, grayer, but a powerful*
man—in a shabby seaman's jacket and cap,
abruptly rushes down stairs into room, his eyes
wild with hate)

JAMES. What's that name you said?!

GWEN. (*blearily, contentedly drinking directly from bottle*) Name? What name? Oh, you mean "Prince Charming" over there?

(JAMES *gives a roar of rage, rushes upon* DORIAN, *and slams him up against left wall, leaning his face fiercely close to the other man's, as MUSIC intros and he sings:*)

JAMES.
So it's you, it's you! We've finally met!
You're the creature who I could never forget!
All those years of searching now are at an end!
Now at last my sister's honor I'll defend!

DORIAN. (*terrified, his face shadowed by hat and collar*)
I am at a disadvantage, sir,
I don't know the sister to whom you refer.
You've mistaken me for someone else, it's plain.

JAMES.
No, I've not! I'm Sybil's brother, James Vane!
Because of you, she took her life,
As if you had plunged in the knife!
For nearly two decades you've been
Escaping the wrath of your sin!
No longer will you have to wait!
Prince Charming, prepare for your fate!

(*maintains hold on* DORIAN's *throat with upstage hand, draws gleaming knife from his belt with the other*)

DORIAN.
Hold on, sir, look closely and see,
A youth such as I couldn't be
The man that you seek for a crime
Committed before my own time!

(JAMES *knocks* DORIAN's *hat off with his knife-hand, sees his face, and starts back in shock, releasing him*)

JAMES.
Good Lord! You are right! It is true!
In no way could it have been you!
Forgive me this awful mistake—
You life I was ready to take!
    DORIAN. (*nervously, anxious to leave quickly*)
Forget it, no harm has been done—
It's late, and I really must run!

(*Grabs up his fallen hat and exits to street;* JAMES *shud-
    ders, sick with what he might have done, and slips
    his knife back into his belt; he staggers to bar,
    shakily pounds his fist upon it*)

JAMES. A drink! Give me a drink! Dear God—what I
might have done!

(*Music plays, now—a mocking parody of the lovesong
    DORIAN once entranced GWEN with—as she moves
    toward JAMES*)

GWEN. He got away. You had him—and you let him
get away.
JAMES. He was the wrong man! Get away from me,
you old hag!
GWEN. (*laughs raucously over SECOND SPATE OF
MOCKING MUSIC; then:*) I wasn't alway this way. He
made me this way . . . a lifetime ago . . .
JAMES. (*looks up*) What's that you say—?!
GWEN. (*not singing, but speaking in time to a
LILTING ECHO OF THE WALTZ she once danced
with* DORIAN)
Dorian Gray hasn't aged in a generation!
Something protects him, he never gets caught!
        (*final chord of MUSIC SUSTAINS, for:*)
JAMES. (*straightening, grim in his determination*) Till
now, dear lady . . . till now!

(*New music intros, as he strides halfway to door, but
    stops to declare in a frenzy at mid-room, singing
    hoarsely:*)
I will track him down, I will seek him out,
I will hack him down where he stands!
Let him try to hide, yet his blood will spout,
And he'll know he died at my hands!
He shall not get away!
I will plot for the day
Mister Dorian Gray   ·
Shall have paid with his life
On the blade of my knife
For the maid he betrayed!
This I vow!

(*He rushes out, slamming door after him;* GWEN *and*
    HAGS *move to soup kettle, swing hob out, and
    hover in a witchlike trio over it, slowly stirring the
    soup, new music intros, and:*)

   TRIO. (*sing*)
Prince Charming, try a taste of trouble!
Bone shall break and blood shall bubble!
Go, tormented sailor, to your work!
Enjoy your just reward, but dearie,
We won't laugh, we're much too weary—
Vengenance seldom smiles—but it can smirk!

(LIGHTS FADE - end of scene)

SCENE 15

The parlor of DORIAN'S *country house. A sofa, an
archway leading to hall, and a large window to one
side of—and slightly to rear of—sofa.* HENRY *is
seated on sofa, happily sipping a brandy;* DORIAN

is standing idly at window, looking out into darkness.

DORIAN. I think they are returning from the hunt, Henry. We really should have joined them, you know.

HENRY. Nonsense! With your excellent cellar and no end of crystal goblets to deplete it with ? I've never enjoyed what they call the "thrill of the hunt"—especially a fox hunt: The unspeakable in pursuit of the uneatable!

DORIAN. (*laughs, turns*) Well, Hetty certainly agrees with you. She did not go, either.

HENRY. A most agreeable young lady. I have adored her company this weekend. Where *is* she now, by the way?

DORIAN. Upstairs, making herself more beautiful, she says—as if such a thing were possible—so that she may play hostess for me at dinner.

HENRY. You are quite taken with her, aren't you, Dorian!

DORIAN. I did not know it was possible to be so much in love, Harry.

HENRY. (*his manner growing more serious*) Is that really all that kept you back from the hunt? Being near Hetty? It has occurred to me this weekend that you are showing an astonishing skill at avoiding going out-of-doors—and you continually stare out whatever window you happen to be near. Are you—expecting anybody?

DORIAN. (*not convincingly*) Of course not, Harry! What a silly thing to suggest! (*sees* HENRY's *look, and adds, with more conviction:*) But I do hate to be away from her—even if she's only in the next room—even if it's only for a few moments—Harry, I adore that woman!

(*MUSIC intros, and he sings:*)
Hetty—my first true love and only love for all my life!
Hetty—I'm dreaming of the moment she becomes my

wife!
She spurs my aching heart to pound beyond control!
Whenever we're apart, it drains my very soul!
Hetty—sweet rain upon the drought—the soothing
   breeze of May—
Hetty—I can't survive without her love another day!
My life was just decay and dust till saved by her love so
   fine . . .
How can I rest till Hetty is mine?!

HENRY. Dorian, dear boy, if you must indluge yourself in rhapsodizing about a beloved, I do wish you wouldn't do so when alone in a room with *me*! What might the servants think!

(*as* DORIAN *laughs,* HETTY *enters the room, brilliantly gowned, and fully as beautiful to us as she is to him*)
Ah, the young lady herself! I shall depart and leave you two to moon at one another unobserved. So much sweetness is bad for my stomach.

HETTY. (*waves him down before he can quite rise*) You shall do no such thing, Harry. We adore your aura of venomous irascibility. It makes the two of us seem so much nicer by contrast!
(HENRY *laughs, and subsides happily with his brandy*) Dear Dorian—(*goes to him, takes his hands*) I cannot tell you how marvelous this weekend has been! This house is so large, with so many beautiful things in it—!

DORIAN. And all of them pale beside your lovely face.

HENRY. Oh, really, now! My stomach can only stand so much, you know. Can you two not forget the pounding of your pulses for the moment, and simply relax and enjoy this life of luxury into which we were born?

HETTY. But it's so tiresome just sitting about.

HENRY. Nonsense! It's the most delightful sensation in the world!
   (*MUSIC intros, and he sings:*)

Oh, the life of the idle rich,
That the persons of privilege tread,
Where there's never a concern
That we'd ever need to learn
What it's like to have to earn our daily bread!
Oh, the life of the idle rich!
Though we could spend it lying abed,
We are gentlefolk by birth,
And as such of greater worth,
So we pass our days on earth in mirth, instead!
    HETTY. (*facetiously joins in for the fun of it*)
We're of the elite, that is true.
Our blood is impeccably blue.
Our clothing's designed
With the wealthy in mind
From the hat to the tip of the shoe.
    DORIAN. (*similarly, not meaning a word of it*)
We know our positions entail
That we dine on the best without fail.
At any old luncheon
We're merrily munchin'
On lobster, roast duckling and quail!
    HENRY.
Though mere wealth doesn't always suffice,
Our existence we find rather nice.
Now, the life of the terribly poor
Has a certain improper allure,
And I could be tempted to
Live in squalor as they do,
If it didn't mean a ruined manicure!
Still, your days would be never humdrum
In a life where you hadn't a crumb;
It's amazing, but I feel
There's a certain strange appeal
Not to know where one's next meal is coming from!

HETTY.
The idea's amusing, of course,
But it's something I dasn't endorse:
To eat bread without butter,
And sleep in the gutter,
Would fill me with utter remorse.
    DORIAN. (*to* HENRY)
If to poverty you should apply,
You must promise me you will drop by.
But you wouldn't come knowing
Your underwear's showing,
So I doubt you're going to try!
    HENRY. (*nods in agreement*)
To forgo triviality's wise,
When we know our reality lies
In the life of the idle rich!
    HETTY. (*starts a mock-minuet step with* DORIAN)
Be it known it's our natural niche!
    DORIAN.
We may find it boring, but—
    DORIAN/HETTY.
For the weary, toilsome rut—
    ALL THREE.
Of the proletariat we'd never switch
From the life of the idle rich!

(*On final phrase,* HENRY *is seated jovially on sofa, still,
    waving his brandy-glass in time to the tempo, while*
    HETTY *and* DORIAN—*she with her back to the win-
    dow—complete their minuet in the usual manner,
    he with a slight bow, she with a deeper curtsey to
    him, so that he facing directly toward window as
    the ferociously glaring face of* JAMES VANE *ap-
    pears there;* DORIAN *gives a loud cry of terror, and
    reels back, falling to the floor;* JAMES *darts away
    immediately*)

HETTY. (*rushes to him, as* HENRY *come to his feet*) Dorian, darling, what is it?! You're pale as death!

DORIAN. (*as she helps him to his feet*) The window—there—I thought I saw—
(HETTY *and* HENRY *are glancing toward the now-empty spot*)
Never mind. It's nothing. A trick of the light. Perhaps I've had too much brandy—or not enough sleep—

HENRY. But, Dorian—what did you imagine you saw there?

DORIAN. A face. A face of a man who means me dreadful harm. But it may have been the mere manifestation of my conscience, of course. (*turns to* HETTY, *takes her hands most sorrowfully*) I do wish I were really the fine fellow you seem to so admire . . . oh, but, my darling, I'm not . . . there are things in my past . . . horrid things . . .

HENRY. Here, now, not another word. You must go and lie down at once. A cool cloth upon your forehead—allow your nerves to recover and relax.

DORIAN. (*nodding, backing toward door*) Yes, yes, that's the very thing I need. Just a few short moments of rest . . . of calm . . .

HETTY. What shall I tell the others—at dinner—?

DORIAN. Oh, I'll be right enough by dinnertime. Truly I will. I just need a short time alone, that is all. I do apologize for upsetting you . . . excuse me . . . (*he exits from room*)

HETTY. My poor darling. (*turns to* HENRY) He *is* a good man, Harry—I feel it, inside—whatever he may think of himself!

HENRY. (*takes her hands*) My dear—I love that man fully as much as you do. But I must tell you—I know from some very personal experience that not all the rumors about him are untrue . . . if you marry him, you will have much unhappiness to share with him. I fear.

HETTY. Has your deeper knowledge of him injured your friendship toward him?

HENRY. No, of course not.

HETTY. Then it shall in no way affect mine.

(DORIAN *appears in an indeterminate locale slightly upstage, supposedly some other room of the house, just standing in weary sorrow in a cone of light, as MUSIC intros, and—*)

HETTY (*sings contrapuntally with the absent*) DORIAN

He's too good to be true!	Something new . . .
Who could not recognize	There's always
The goodness shining through	Something new . . .
His bright unclouded eyes!	A dusting
The stories told about him	Of depravity . . .
Cannot be the truth,	Or soft decay . . .
For his glorious outward glow	To greet me each new day
Of unspotted youth disproves the lies,	As I scan the canvas
And make my heart despise	There in
Any who doubt him!	Fearful
How dare they criticize?	View . . .
Why must a woman wait	Then I stand with a mirror
In cumbersome decorum?	In my trembling hand,
I'll not hesitate!	And I peer into the glass
I'll lay my heart before him!	Only to see
Why should I hide the raking	A youthful face, and I

Pain each time we part? Sigh in relief, as the
I must confide the aching Curtaining cloth upon the
Hunger in my heart! Fiend I replace . . .
A future fair and fine Then I do
Together we'll pursue! Anything
Oh, Dorian, be mine! I'm longing to . . .
Oh, darling, if you knew Till the dawn
The saintliness I view in When I renew
 you!
You're too good The crumbling view
To be true! Of something new . . .!

(she stands in rapture, and he sags in despair, as—)

(LIGHTS FADE - end of scene)

SCENE 16

A field near the woods on DORIAN's *estate. Generally barren, but with some frost-dusted shrubs [the all-white decor should make them look exactly right, here] at the center stage and upstage areas.* BOYCE, BEECHMONT *and* ELLERTON, *in hunting togs, carrying shotguns, are standing in a group to one side;* HENRY *and* DORIAN, *overcoated and hatted, enter from opposite side.*

BOYCE. Ho, there, Dorian! Good to see you out of the house!

ELLERTON. These frosty mornings do wonders for the complexion.

BEECHMONT. But where is your fowling-piece?

DORIAN. I am here merely as an observer, Lady Beechmont.

HENRY. And I as his unwilling prisoner. Why any decently brought-up person should want to arise at such a dreadful hour to match wits with a partridge is beyond my understanding!

ELLERTON. *Pour le sport,* Harry, *pour le sport!* (*the French phrase is pronounced "POOR LUH SPOR"*)

HENRY. And what is so sporting in propelling a thousand particles of lead at one tiny dimwitted bird?

BOYCE. Oh, Harry, where's your sense of adventure?!

ELLERTON. Of challenge!

BEECHMONT. Of excitement!

DORIAN. Of suspense!

          (*MUSIC intros, and—*)

FOURSOME. (*sing, to an amusingly unconvinced* HENRY:)

At cracking of dawn to the marshes we go,
Through bracken and brush over shimmering snow,
Till silence is rent by a rifle's report—!
Heigh-ho for a jolly good sport!

The breach of the barrel, the click of the lock,
The crack of the cartridge, the fluttering flock,
The smell of the smoke and the fall of the prey—!
Heigh-ho for a jolly good day!
(*Group points to something offstage, moving their arms
      in a simultaneous horizontal arc toward center
      stage, as if tracking the progress of a small scurry-
      ing animal*)
The beaters have routed a rabbit, I think!
Be quick, now, or he'll be away in a wink!
    (*all are now pointing toward center-stage shrub*)
He's taken to cover, don't scare him, be still—!
    (TRIO *beside* DORIAN *raise shotguns and aim*)
Heigh-ho for a jolly good kill!

(*On final note of song,* TRIO *all fire toward shrub, and—with a loud cry of agony—*JAMES VANE *rears up into view from behind shrub, his chest a bloody horror, his mouth open in shock, his eyes wide with pain and suprise; then he topples backward, arms flung wide, out of sight*)

BOYCE. (*as* ALL *rush partway upstage to look down on unseen body*) Good lord, we've hit a beater!
ELLERTON. No, that's not one of the beaters!
BEECHMONT. He seems to be a sort of seafaring man!
HENRY. Lord Boyce, see to the ladies! I'll return to the house and send someone to fetch a doctor!

(HENRY *exits, fast, and* BOYCE *escorts* ELLERTON *and* BEECHMONT *offstage after him, at a slower pace, during:*)

ELLERTON. This has absolutely ruined my morning!
BEECHMONT. Now, now, don't blame yourself. The man was obviously a trespasser!
BOYCE. A damned fool, if you ask me, to go skulking about during a shoot!

(*They are gone;* DORIAN *remains where he has stood since moving up beyond the shrub, just staring down upon the fallen man with a look of pity and deep unhappiness*)

DORIAN. James Vane. I should feel elation and relief—but I only feel sorrow and despair. You were right to come after me, you know. I deserved to die. You did not. Well—you are with your sweet sister, now—commend me to her. She suffered much at my hands. Far too much.

(*Buries his face in his hands and sobs; as he does so,* HETTY *rushes onstage from the direction the others departed, her face grave with concern; she takes his arm*)

HETTY. Dorian! My sweet Dorian! You must not let this grieve you so! His death was no fault of yours!

DORIAN. (*looks at her, smiling ruefully*) Ah, but it was, my dear. Shall I tell you who this man was? He was the brother of a girl I wronged most cruelly, many years ago. It was *his* face I saw at the window yesternight. He was here to kill me. I dearly wish he had.

HETTY. (*embraces him, afraid*) My darling, you must not say such things!

DORIAN. Oh, Hetty, don't you understand?! I am vile, the lowest creature that crawls upon the face of the earth. Do not be deceived by my outward appearance. If you knew my soul, you would be fleeing in revulsion!

HETTY. No! No, I will not believe such things of you! You are fine, and good, and desperate for happiness! Let me be your happiness! Let me be your wife!

DORIAN. Wife?! My love would contaminate you! I care for you far too much to sully your goodness with the stains of my lifetime of sins!

HETTY. But don't you see?! You abominate your past! It repels you! If that is not goodness, I know not what is!

DORIAN. I am only repelled by my soul's ugliness. I am past repentance.

HETTY. Do not say such things! Everyone has dark deeds that cloud the sweetness of the past! Even I—!

DORIAN. (*smiles at her tenderly, wonderingly*) You? My heavenly angel? My only delight? I cannot believe it.

HETTY. But it is true. There is something about me which, if you knew it, would shock you, make you abandon me in horror.

DORIAN. (*takes her face tenderly in his hands*) My darling, for nothing in *your* past would I forsake you—only for the hideous secrets of my *own*!

HETTY. Then let me share my secret with you! It will make us kindred spirits! Darkness attracted to darkness! I am not all that I claim to be!

DORIAN. Hetty, Hetty, I tell you that there is nothing you could reveal which would change the abiding love for you in my heart of hearts!

HETTY. (*takes a backstep from him, braces herself; then:*) Then I would have you know that I am not the highborn lady you imagine me to be. My supposed parents, the Duvals, could not have children of their own—I am the bastard child of an unfortunate woman they knew and loved—they carried this secret to their graves.

DORIAN. (*afraid to believe what has occured to him, but must know*) And—this woman—this friend—my darling Hetty—who was she?

HETTY. The unfortunate daughter of Lady Margaret Langdon—Gwendolyn Langdon.

DORIAN. (*stares at her in horror*) Gwen! You are Gwen's daughter! And that means—that means—

HETTY. Means what, my darling? Why do you look upon me with such pain?

DORIAN. Dear God! I am fully punished for my crimes at last! This is the crowning irony, the bitterest horror! (*backs from her*) Oh, Hetty—Hetty—we can never be wed—it is over for us—it is all over—finished! (*turns violently away and rushes off*)

HETTY. (*shocked*) Dorian! Dorian—! (*and as she stands there in heartbroken bewilderment—*)

(*LIGHTS FADE - end of scene*)

SCENE 17

DORIAN's *parlor/attic, fully lighted.* DORIAN *enters from hall, tearing off his overcoat and flinging it aside as he rushes up the stairs to confront the covered portrait, from which he now yanks the cloth, letting it dangle from the upper corner of the frame. He stares at the misshappen creature there, panting with fury and despair.*

DORIAN. Monster! Hideous monster! To this miserable end have you brought me! Hetty—my own daughter! I cannot abide it! I will not! She shall never know the depths of my depravity! I will destroy you first! (*snatches up same knife with which he murdered* BASIL) Do not smile your mocking lips at me! I know I have abjured you in the past—but that was mere vanity on my part, disgust with your lack of beauty! This time it is hatred—for all you are—for all that your horror represents! I despise my foolish wish of so many years past! I loathe the sight of you. I pray God I can find the strength and courage to destroy you! It will be the one shining deed in an otherwise worthless life!
          (*MUSIC intros, and he sings:*)
For once, I'll do something that's decent,
That's truly worthwhile.
A new life begins on this very day,
As I flee the ways I despise!
Perhaps my reform is too recent
To change all that's vile,
That etches the sins of my sordid past
In the picture's dastardly guise.
But some day I'll look upon with dignity
The picture of Dorian Gray . . .
I must put an end to my malignity!
May God help me find my way!
For once in my life I'll be free of
The fiend on my wall!
For I now realize, when the portrait dies,
That my soul can arise from its fall . . .

I can do it, for once . . . and for all!

(*raises dagger to stab portrait, then stops as* HETTY *rushes in from hall, below, throwing aside her cloak, and he hears:*)

HETTY. Dorian! Dorian!
(*she sees his overcoat flung down upon the stairs, starts past it and up them in a frantic rush*)
DORIAN. (*shocked*) Hetty! Coming up here! (*drops dagger*)
HETTY. (*ascending, her voice heartbroken*)
My darling, where are you? I need you!
My darling, my own!
DORIAN. (*whirls, frantically re-covering portrait*)
Dear God! Don't let her see this!
HETTY. (*nearing top of stairs*)
Dorian, darling! Where are you?
Oh, why have you flown?
DORIAN. (*slumps in resignation*)
Perhaps the time has come to fall upon
My knees and let her know the reason . . .
    (*she has arrived; he steps to her, takes her hands*)
Hetty! Dear Hetty!
I love you so madly!
HETTY. (*uncertainly, but relieved to find him*)
Then why stare so sadly?
Come here to my arms!
                    (*they embrace*)
DORIAN.
My dear, I care for you so much!
Oh, hold me near!
HETTY.
I'm here! Take comfort in my nearness,
In my touch!
BOTH.
Within your sweet embrace, I'm truly blessed—

DORIAN.
So truly blessed—
BOTH.
With love so diff'rent—
HETTY.
Oh—
BOTH.
So diff'rent from the rest—!

(*She moves her face upward to kiss him; he almost
    responds, then with horror pushes her away, turns
    away*)

DORIAN.
No! I can't do such a thing to you!
Not to you!
HETTY.
But, oh, my darling,
My heart is just aching to share
The trouble you're in !
DORIAN.
Is it possible—?
HETTY.
It's time to begin!
DORIAN.
This could be the time—!
HETTY.
Whatever has been—
DORIAN.
With a love like hers—!
HETTY.
I don't care!
DORIAN.
I wonder if I dare reveal
The terrifying truth . . .
HETTY.
What truth?

DORIAN.
About . . .
  HETTY.
What?
  DORIAN.
The picture!
  HETTY.
Darling . . .
  DORIAN.
The horror of the picture and me!
  HETTY.
You're not even making sense!
  DORIAN.
Darling, you see—
  HETTY.
How can a picture harm us?
  DORIAN.
I am not free!
  HETTY.
What picture could alter—
  DORIAN.
I've got to make you understand—!
  HETTY.
What my heart sees in you
Or make me falter—
  DORIAN.
What?
  DORIAN/HETTY.
No matter what you're/I'm going to view?!
  HETTY.
Show me, now!
  DORIAN.
Can it be true?
  HETTY.
My dearest darling, I love you—

DORIAN.
The choice is made!
HETTY.
Whatever may be!
DORIAN.
Far too late to now turn away!
HETTY.
In that picture, remember,
Whatever I see—
DORIAN.
The price I've paid for my state,
You shall learn today!
 (*moves to take hold of cloth at right edge of portrait*)
HETTY.
My love will never die!
DORIAN.
Behind this cloth, you'll behold—
HETTY.
Whatever you may do—
DORIAN.
Something hideous and old!
HETTY.
Remember I'm in love . . .
DORIAN.
It is my soul I've sold . . .!
HETTY.
With . . .
DORIAN. (*a shout of despair*)
For this!

(*Music continues under remainder of dialogue, as*
    DORIAN *steps to one side of the portrait, pulling*
    the cloth free from the canvas as he does so, thus
    revealing the picture, and—because the cloth re-
    mains attached to the upper left corner of the
    frame—simultaneously concealing himself: and the

picture is as we first saw it! It is young Dorian, in the full bloom of his youth and beauty!)

HETTY. I don't understand . . . ?

(*And as she stares at the lovely portrait, the cloth drops from in front of* DORIAN—*and* THE MONSTER *from the canvas stands there, in all his repellent horror, staring at her*)

HETTY. (*recoils with a shriek of terror*) Aaaaah—!
MONSTER. (*moves toward her, hands outstretched, croaking horribly:*) Hetty!
HETTY. (*backing from him, toward open window*) Who *are* you?
MONSTER. Don't you know me?
HETTY. *What* are you? Dorian, where are you?
MONSTER. (*sees she is at brink of open window, rushes at her*) Hetty!
HETTY. Help me!
(*topples backward through open window, and we immediately see her—via the tall downstairs window—hurtle headlong down to the street and her death [see SPECIAL EFFECTS], on:*)
Aaaaah—!
MONSTER. (*abruptly sees his own outstretched hands shrieks:*) Oh, no—! (*turns and sees restored portrait, groans softly:*) No—! (*grabs up hand-mirror and sees his face, sighs weakly:*) No—! Hetty—! Dear God— forgive me!

(*crumples, falls dead upon the floor before the portrait, and music moves on to tragic climax as lights dim swiftly on everything, until only the the painting can be seen, in all its pristine beauty, then it, too, fades from view, as—*)

THE CURTAIN FALLS

—End of Show—

—SPECIAL EFFECTS—

1) The picture. The frame is actually the front end of a rectangular box, its sides and top dead black, at the interior rear of which are mounted a pair of slide-projectors, hooked by rheostat so that as the current increases the light of one, it decreases the light of the other, and projected "portrait" can change smoothly through all its phases (such as the opening of Scene 10) as if by magic. The "canvas" itself is a black *Roscoscreen,* which shows high-contrast rear-projected pictures even with stage lights on the front of it. (The Portrait shown in the opening scene of the show, on the easel, is of course an actual painting, as is the one in Scene Seven.)

2) The monster. This is another actor, garbed in the soiled clothing as seen in the altered portrait, and in either grotesque makeup or a head-covering hideous rubber mask and monster-hands, who changes places with Dorian in the few moments he is behind the cloth. The actor portraying Alan/James is probably the best one to use the this; and the mask is preferable to makeup in that it allows a faster change for the player, and easy removal for the curtain call.

3) Hetty's death. This is achieved simply by having a sturdy platform outside the attic window, beneath which is a dummy garbed precisely as Hetty is, keyed to be released automatically the moment she lands upon the (padded, we hope for her sake) Platform itself. This dummy should be mounted so that its heels rest upon a support, so that when the upper torso is released, it will fall before the feet themselves start down, giving the impression that her backward-topple is continuing its arc, allowing her a headfirst-plunge (back to us) to the unseen pavement. The effects upon the audience in this final scene should be devastating, with its triple-shocks: Seeing the young portrait, seeing the monster, and then seeing Hetty's plunge.

—A NOTE ON MAKEUP—

The period in which the play occurs allows us the luxury of having, or not having, sideburns, beards, moustaches, etc., on the male players. In this way, Alan, for instance, can be short-haired with a light moustache, whereas his alter-ego James can have a clean upper lip but wear a seaman's beard (one that covers cheeks and chin but *not* the upper lip), so that the two will look like different persons. And the dark/auburn/blonde hair of Sybil/Gwen/Hetty will serve to differentiate among them all quite nicely. Similar alterations in hair, facial hair, and color of hair, will easily differentiate all the other players in their various roles, for maximum large-cast effect.

PROMENADE, ALL!
DAVID V. ROBISON

(Little Theatre) Comedy
3 Men, 1 Woman, Interior

Four actors play four successive generations of the same family, as their business grows from manufacturing buttons to a conglomerate of international proportions (in the U.S. their perfume will be called Belle Nuit; but in Paris, Enchanted Evening). The Broadway cast included Richard Backus, Anne Jackson, Eli Wallach and Hume Cronyn. Miss Jackson performed as either mother or grandmother, as called for; and Cronyn and Wallach alternated as fathers and grandfathers; with Backus playing all the roles of youth. There are some excellent cameos to perform, such as the puritanical mother reading the Bible to her son without realizing the sexual innuendoes; or the 90-year-old patriarch who is agreeable to trying an experiment in sexology but is afraid of a heart attack.

> "So· likeable; jolly and splendidly performed."—*N.Y. Daily News.* "The author has the ability to write amusing lines, and there are many of them."—*N.Y. Post.* "Gives strong, lively actors a chance for some healthy exercise. And what a time they have at it!"—*CBS-TV.*

ROYALTY, $50-$35

ACCOMMODATIONS
NICK HALL

(Little Theatre) Comedy
2 Men, 2 Women, Interior

Lee Schallert, housewife, feeling she may be missing out on something, leaves her husband, Bob, and her suburban home and moves into a two-room Greenwich Village apartment with two roommates. One roommate, Pat, is an aspiring actress, never out of characters or costumes, but, through an agency mix up, the other roommate is a serious, young, graduate student—male. The ensuing complications make a hysterical evening.

> "An amusing study of marital and human relations . . . a gem . . . It ranks as one of the funniest ever staged."—*Labor Herald.* "The audience at Limestone Valley Dinner Theater laughed at "Accommodations" until it hurt."—*News American.* "Superior theater, frivolous, perhaps, but nonetheless superior. It is light comedy at its best."—*The Sun, Baltimore.*

ROYALTY, $50-$25

COUNT DRACULA

TED TILLER

(All Groups) Mystery comedy
7 Men, 2 Women. Interior with Small Inset
1930 Costumes (optional)

Based on Bram Stoker's 19th Century novel, "Dracula." This is a new, witty version of the classic story of a suave vampire whose passion is sinking his teeth into the throats of beautiful young women. Mina, his latest victim, is the ward of Dr. Seward in whose provincial insane asylum the terrifying action transpires. Her finance arrives from London, worried over her strange inertia and trance-like state. Equally concerned is Professor Van Helsing, specialist in rare maladies, who senses the supernatural at work. Added trouble comes from Sybil, Dr. Sewards demented, sherry-tippling sister and from Renfield, a schizophrenic inmate in league with the vampire. But how to trap this ghoul who can transform himself into a bat, materialize from fog, dissolve in mist? There are many surprising but uncomplicated stage effects, mysterious disappearances, secret panels, howling wolves, bats that fly over the audience, an unexpected murder, and magic tricks which include Dracula's vanishing in full view of the spectators.

Despite much gore, ". . . the play abounds with funny lines. There is nothing in it but entertainment."—*Springfield, Mass. News.*

ROYALTY, $50-$25

FRANKENSTEIN

TIM KELLY

(All Groups)
4 Men, 4 Women, Interior

Victor Frankenstein, a brilliant young scientist, returns to his chateau on the shores of Lake Geneva to escape some terrible pursuer. No one can shake free the dark secret that terrifies him. Not his mother, nor his financee Elizabeth, nor his best friend, Henry Clerval. Even the pleading of a gypsy girl accused of murdering Victor's younger brother falls on deaf ears, for Victor has brought into being a "Creature" made from bits and pieces of the dead! The Creature tracks Victor to his sanctuary to demand a bride to share its loneliness—one as wretched as the Creature itself. Against his better judgment, Victor agrees and soon the household is invaded by murder, despair and terror! The play opens on the wedding night of Victor and Elizabeth, the very time the Creature has sworn to kill the scientist for destroying its intended mate, and ends, weeks later, in a horrific climax of dramatic suspense! In between there is enough macabre humor to relieve the mounting tension. Perhaps the truest adaptation of Mary Shelley's classic yet. Simple to stage and a guaranteed audience pleaser.

ROYALTY, $25.00

A COMMUNITY OF TWO
JEROME CHODOROV

(All Groups) Comedy
4 Men, 3 Women, Interior

Winner of a Tony Award for "Wonderful Town." Co-author of "My Sister Eileen," "Junior Miss," "Anniversary Waltz." This is a charming off-beat comedy about Alix Carpenter, a fortyish divorceè of one month who has been locked out of her own apartment and is rescued by her thrice-divorced neighbor across the hall, Michael Jardeen. During the course of the two hours in which it takes to play out the events of the evening, we meet Alix's ex-husband, a stuffed shirt from Wall Street, her son, who has run away from prep school with his girl, heading for New Mexico and a commune. Michael's current girl friend, Olga, a lady anthropologist just back from Lapland, and Mr. Greenberg, a philosopher-locksmith. All take part in the hilarious doings during a blizzard that rages outside the building and effects everybody's lives. But most of all, and especially, we get to know the eccentric Michael Jardeen, and the confused and charming Alix Carpenter, who discover that love might easily happen, even on a landing, in the course of a couple of hours of highstress living.

"Thoroughly delightful comedy."—*St. Louis-Post Dispatch.* "A joy."—*Cleveland Plain Dealer.* "Skillful fun by Jerome Chodorov."—*Toronto Globe Star.*

ROYALTY, $50-$35

ROMAN CONQUEST
JOHN PATRICK

(All Groups) Comedy
One set—3 Women, 6 Men

The romantic love story of two American girls living in the romantic city of Rome in a romantic garret at the foot of the famous Spanish steps. One of the world's richest young women takes her less fortunate girl friend to Italy to hide unknown and escape notoriety while she attempts to discover if she has any talent as an artist—free of position and prestige. Their misadventures with language and people supply a delightful evening of pure entertainment. Remember the movies "Three Coins in the Fountain" and "Love Is A Many Splendored Thing"? This new comedy is in the same vein by the same Pulitzer Prize winning playwright.

ROYALTY, $50-$35